PARENTS AND CHURCH LEADERS GUIDE

CHRISTIAN

S · E · X

EDUCATION

JIMMY HESTER, COMPILER

FamilyTouch.

Nashville, Tennessee

Reprinted 1993.

7810-43
ISBN: 0-8054-9970-9

Dewey Decimal Classification: 613.907
Subject Heading: SEX EDUCATION
Printed in the United States of America

Unless otherwise noted, Scripture quotations are from the King James Version of the Bible.

Scripture quotations marked NIV are from the Holy Bible, *New International Version,* copyright © 1973, 1978, 1984 by International Bible Society.

Scripture quotations marked NASB are from the *New American Standard Bible.* © The Lockman Foundation, 1960, 1962, 1963, 1968, 1971, 1972, 1973, 1975, 1977. Used by permission.

Family Touch Press
127 Ninth Avenue, North
Nashville, TN 37234

Preface

Parenting is a divine trust. As Christian parents, we are responsible for modeling, living, and teaching our children the Christian faith and imparting Christian values to them. We are to love, care for, protect, train, and guide our children (Eph. 6:4). Principles for rearing children are found in the Bible; skills based on these principles are developed by each generation.

Our responsibility for nurturing and teaching our children includes the physical, mental, social, emotional, and spiritual aspects of living. Family life needs a moral and spiritual foundation. God created persons in His image and instituted the family as a crucial arena for human growth and fulfillment.

God created us male and female, sexual beings. The Bible is clear that sexuality is created and ordained by God. Human sexuality is a gift, and is meant to be a good part of our human experience. Sexuality is the quality of possessing maleness and femaleness, and is inherent in our human personality. Our sexuality is expressed in many ways other than sexual intercourse, but sexual intercourse is an important expression of sexual intimacy and is to be reserved for the one-flesh relationship of marriage. Sexual intercourse is intended for that relationship in which a man and a woman commit themselves to each other in responsible love (Gen. 1:26-28).

Sexual activity among children and youth is epidemic. Most surveys of U.S. teenagers indicate that more than half have had intercourse by the time they are seventeen years old. In an attempt to respond to this crisis, a number of school systems and other agencies have initiated sex education, most not inclusive of biblical principles and ideas. By design, their curriculum is more informational in its orientation, and targeted to the teenage years. Some even distribute birth control devices to prevent pregnancy, and to prevent AIDS and sexually-transmitted diseases.

Traditionally, we have not been willing to discuss sexual issues, even with our own children. Often, we may not know how to respond as parents to the openness in our society when such openness was not prevalent in our early life. The results of this openness and freedom of sexual expression has resulted in a moral and ethical decline in our time. We are frightened by the world we see in which we are rearing our children.

Sex education should happen at home, although we must admit that most parents feel uncomfortable talking about sex. Because of this, many of us are doing nothing. Thus the reason for this Christian Sex Education series. The books in this series are unique; they are books you can trust. Why? These resources . . .

• Assist you as a parent to rear mature, responsible Christian children who apply biblical principles of sexuality in their everyday living.

• Promote abstinence, chastity, healthy self-esteem, and self-discipline among unmarried children and teenagers.

• Assist you and your church to lead children and teenagers to understand the good that God intended for sexual intercourse within marriage and encourage them to enjoy this relationship only within a God-ordained covenant marriage.

• Teach appreciation for one's body as God-created and the responsibility each person has to maintain appropriate boundaries with others, and minister to children and teenagers who have fallen short of God's ideal for sexual relationships.

• Provide well-tested, reliable, and effective materials for you and your church to educate your children about sexuality and how God intends for it to be expressed.

This parents and church leaders guide is foundational to the Christian Sex Education series. The books in this series were designed based on the assumption that Christian parents have the responsibility to teach their children the foundational truths about sexuality. Thus, the heart of this guide is the section, "Parents Providing Christian Sex Education." This section will help you identify and apply biblical teachings related to Christian sex education. The section will equip you to understand and appreciate your children's development, and to understand their age-related learning abilities. You will be given guidance in how to use Christian sex education resources with children and teenagers.

The church plays a supportive role. The section, "Church Leaders Supporting Parents," offers a plan for training and orienting parents in using the series with their children and teenagers. Supplementary group session plans supported by parental involvement for leading preadolescents and adolescents through the Christian Sex Education resources are provided.

We selected quality writers for this guide. Their professional expertise along with their commitment to assist you as a parent make this a resource you will refer to often. May we introduce them to you . . .

Bill Blackburn, pastor of Trinity Baptist Church, Kerrville, Texas, has written extensively in the area of family life.

Michael Fink is manager of the Adult Life and Work/VBS Curriculum Section, Church Growth/Sunday School Division, Baptist Sunday School Board, Nashville, Tennessee.

Wilson Wayne Grant, M.D., a pediatrician practicing in San Antonio, Texas, has written several books and "Your Teen's Health," a feature in *Living with Teenagers*, since the magazine began fifteen years ago.

Susan Lanford is a family life conference leader, speaker, and writer from Nashville, Tennessee, having written *Remarriage and Blended Family Workshop*.

Ellen Chambers is Minister of Preschool and Children at First Baptist Church, Lewisville, Texas. She has written for *Beginning* and *Preschoolers at Church* curriculum materials.

Norma Stevens is professor of education at Belmont University, Nashville, Tennessee. Among her publications is the equipping center module, *Helping Children Cope with Crises*.

Ann Cannon is from Atlanta, Georgia, and has written many articles and books on youth issues, including *Bible Teaching for Youth Through the Sunday School*.

Carolyn Jenkins is Minister of Youth and College Students at First Baptist Church, Nashville, Tennessee.

May God richly bless you as you rear your children to become models for their peers and proponents of sexual abstinence until marriage. We cannot be responsible for things beyond our control, but we can accept responsibility for what God has entrusted to us—our children.

Jimmy Hester, Design Editor
Discipleship and Family Development
Baptist Sunday School Board

Contents

Parents and Church Leaders Providing Christian Sex Education

Bill Blackburn

Why is talking with children and youth about sex so hard for most adults? The answer to that question will be dealt with in detail in "Knowing Who You Are as a Parent" later in this book, but for now consider the following response.

The sense is of an invasion of privacy—ours and theirs. Sexual matters are private matters, and we are just not accustomed to talking about them, especially to those younger than us, and especially to our own children.

Embarrassment is also a factor. Most of us have mixed feelings about our bodies and our sexuality. What is appropriate to talk about and what is inappropriate? What if we are asked an embarrassing question? What if we are asked something we don't know and are embarrassed we don't know?

Strong feelings from our past affect our views of sexuality and our views of what is appropriate or inappropriate. Some things we are presently experiencing cause some discomfort in talking about sexual matters.

Perhaps we are hesitant to pass on information about sexual matters because we have no role model for doing so. If no one provided us with the information we needed, we can feel uneasy in these uncharted waters.

Finally, we may feel hesitant about this venture of sex education because we are afraid that we will only give ideas to our children or youth that will prompt them to experiment.

The Importance of Christian Sex Education

Even though some of these are legitimate reasons, we must not let them stand in our way as we pass on information and values about human sexuality. We must educate our children for the following reasons.

1. We live in a sexually explicit society. We need only to look at our television shows, our daily newspapers, and the magazines that come into our homes to know that our children live in a world that bombards them with sexual messages. Our children need to learn how to critically view these messages from the Christian perspective of human sexuality and relationships.

2. Training in sexuality is imperative for the future. If we seek to train the next generation in Christian discipleship and fail to train them in how a Christian disciple is to view sex, then we have failed in our task of training by neglecting this central facet of who we are as persons.

3. We must arm our children with good information. The apostle Paul declared that the Christian must be well-armed and prepared for the battles he or she will face in the world (see Eph. 6:10-18). If our children are to be well armed, they must have good information about their sexual development. For an eleven-year-old boy not to know about what is happening to him with the changes puberty brings, leaves him vulnerable to fear, misinterpretation, misinformation, and exploitation. Not knowing what she may face as she begins dating is to send a fifteen-year-old girl defenseless into what may well turn into a sexual battle.

4. We draw closer in our relationship with our children. Sharing with our children about these matters can develop a closeness. It lets them know we are willing to face the hesitation to talk about sexuality because we consider it important for them to know, and that we do it because we love them. As the child approaches puberty and after, it becomes more difficult to honestly discuss sexual issues. Little appreciation will be forthcoming from the youth, but the appreciation is there and will probably be expressed only much later.

If this issue of imparting values and information about sexuality is so important, then how can we go about it?

Some Essentials to Christian Sex Education

1. Begin with prayer. Pray to the Lord for wisdom, guidance, and timing. Ask God to help you deal with your own feelings about your sexual identity and how it developed, and especially the difficulties you had along the way.

I am reminded of a young mother who had never told anyone about being fondled by her uncle when she was six years old. That incident left her feeling embarrassed, confused, and afraid. The uncle had threatened her if she ever told what happened. Almost 20 years later, she finally told some Christian friends about the incident and how it had made her feel. She at last told her secret because she knew that she was conveying to her own daughter fearful messages about what could happen to her as a little girl and that this had become her dominant message to her four-year-old daughter about sexuality. The

Christian friends, some of whom had had similar experiences, prayed with her. The young mother was now freed to be more open and more positive with her daughter. Plus the shame of her "secret" had lost much of its power over her because it had now been shared.

In honesty before the Lord, we need to pray about our own sense of sexuality. In some instances, we need to seek forgiveness and cleansing before the Lord. We need to thank the Lord for His gift of sexuality to us, however ambivalent we may have been about it at times, or how we may have misused it, or how others might have abused our sexuality.

2. We need to have a sure foundation of biblical teaching on sexuality. The material presented in this resource can provide that. This can be supplemented with your own study of the Scripture plus Christian books on the subject. What a powerful lesson for children and youth when parents and church leaders show them what the Bible teaches about sexuality and how the Bible is a guide to making good decisions in this area of life.

3. In addition to the scriptural teaching on a Christian ethic of sexuality, we need to be equipped with good information about the anatomy and sexual development. You perhaps know the old story of the fourth grader writing a school paper who asked his father how he was born. His father told him the stork brought him. The boy was told the same story from his mother and grandmother about their births. He wrote in his paper, "There hasn't been a natural birth in our family for three generations!" This fourth grader was looking for information and did not buy the misinformation he got in his quest.

Whether they ask or we take the initiative to tell our children about sexual matters, we need to have good information. Where do you get that information? This series of materials on Christian sex education can provide that information.

Most of us grew up with a lot of wrong information about our sexuality and the sexuality of the opposite sex. We gleaned that misinformation from wrong interpretations of what we saw and heard. We gathered it from stories told by our friends. We may have collected it from books and magazines. Perhaps we got it from our parents and other authority figures. But regardless of where we learned our information, we need to have good information to pass on to our children.

4. Knowledge of child development is extremely important when talking with children and youth about sexuality. How you answer a four-year-old's question will be different from answering the question of a fifteen-year-old. If we can understand and remember what may be going through the mind of the one asking the question, we are ahead in being able to answer appropriately.

Along with the good material in this book, do not overlook your own memory of growing up as a resource in understanding children and youth. Do you remember your own sense of curiosity and the questions you had about sexual matters when you were a six-year-old? Do you remember the kinds of things fourteen-year-old girls talked about when sex was the topic? Even more important, do you remember what it felt like to be ten or eleven and have your body change in ways that made you self-conscious and embarrassed? Or do you remember as a high school student all the theories about different ways someone could get pregnant and the different ways to be able to prevent pregnancy?

Several studies have indicated that adults may be willing to talk about events in their childhood and youth, but they are more reluctant to talk about what they felt in those years. Why is that? Probably because we do not care to remember the emotional issues we faced as we grew up. Too many of those are painful. But to empathize with today's children and youth requires us to explore to some measure not only the facts but also the feelings of our growing up years, including the growing pains.

5. To be effective educators about sexual issues, we need to be good communicators. We need to learn when to listen and when to talk. We need to learn how to listen to the language of behavior. We need to know how to discover what is being asked and what is not. We need to sense how much information is enough and when enough is enough. We can learn to sense or explore what is behind the question or comment.

The story is told of the little girl who asked her mother where she came from. Her mother seized the teachable moment and explained to her the "facts of life." After much talking by the mother, accompanied by the silence of the daughter, the mother finally asked, "Why did you want to know where you came from?" The little girl replied, "Well, Cara said she came from South Platte, and Chris said he came from Yuma, and I just wanted to know where I came from." It is important to know what is being asked before we answer the question!

6. The most powerful influence we have on children and youth about sexuality is what we model. In subtle and not so subtle ways, we communicate how we feel about our own sexuality and our values related to relationships between the sexes. In how we dress, how we carry ourselves, what we talk about, and how we treat the opposite sex, we are modeling our views and values of human sexuality. Our self-image as male or female is apparent.

Therefore, a crucial step in Christian sex education involves some self-examination about what we are modeling. This takes us back to the issue of prayer and coming before the Lord for self-examination, confession, and recommitment.

A powerful example of what influences what we model to others relates to our history of relationships with the opposite sex. If there have been or are some damaging relationships, we are likely to convey negative images of persons of the other sex. For instance, a woman working with men who are abusive, inconsiderate, and chauvinistic and who is married to a man who refuses to carry his load around the house, must be on guard against conveying the idea that all men are this way, while at the same time helping a daughter be realistic and helping a son learn to respect women.

In the same way, parents who value and respect each other, are considerate of each other and see each other as persons rather than sexual objects, are modeling for both sons and daughters a powerful image of good relations between the sexes.

Given the power of what we model about sexuality and values related to it, the time must come when we talk about sexual issues as well. This begins when the child is still an infant. While diapering or bathing a child and at other times, we are conveying, both verbally and nonverbally, our attitudes about sexuality. By teaching children the correct names for the parts of their bodies, we are providing them language that is appropriate for any age level. We are to teach the naturalness and beauty of God's creation of us as sexual beings.

In childhood, the appropriate answer to questions is a prime way of communicating both information and values about sexuality. Before children have learned to feel embarrassed about asking questions about sex is a wonderful time of teachable moments. As children begin to enter school, embarrassment and laughter, and sometimes shame and mystery, begin to be associated with talk about sexual matters.

Here the question of initiative comes in. Parents often ask, "What if the child never asks any questions?" Then it is important that you take the initiative, especially prior to key stages in their development (entering school, beginning puberty, and starting romantic involvements).

The summer after my son turned ten, we took a trip to see his favorite baseball team, the New York Yankees, play the Texas Rangers. On the trip back I knew I had a golden opportunity to talk with him about some changes and questions he would soon be facing. I summoned my courage on that five-hour trip, and finally, about sixty miles away from home, I started talking. I covered a number of subjects being careful to remember some of the things I had faced at his age and some of the questions I had had. Carter was silent. He didn't say a word as he looked straight ahead at the road. Did he have any questions? "No." "Are you sure?" "I'm sure." I let him know that anytime he did, I wanted him to feel free to come talk to me. Still frozen in place with eyes fixed straight ahead, he declared he would. Yes, my hunch is I will have to take the initiative again.

Modeling, answering questions, and taking the initiative to deliver information is important, but having and using good resources is also important. How can you use the resources in this series on Christian sex education?

Using These Resources with Your Children

This Christian Sex Education series has been designed first and foremost to be used by the parent in the home. The church can provide a one-time training and orientation session to introduce parents to the material. Beyond that, parents may choose to meet occasionally in a support group format to discuss issues related to their experiences. But the focus of this Christian Sex Education series is for parents to use with their children and youth in the home.

The section of this book, "Parents Providing Christian Sex Education," will help parents as they teach their children. The section, "Church Leaders Supporting Parents," will help churches provide training and support for parents. This section also contains teaching suggestions for churches in which parents encourage their preadolescents and adolescents to participate in supplementary group study at church.

Which Resource Is Best For My Child?

As a parent, you will need to determine which of the four resources for children and youth best fit the needs of your child at his or her present stage of development. The four resources in the series are:

Boys and Girls—Alike and Different by Ellen Chambers (For Young Children)
My Body and Me by Norma Stevens (For Middle-Aged Children)
Sex! What's That? by Susan Lanford (For Preadolescents)
Sexuality: God's Gift by Ann Cannon (For Adolescents)

Even though an age range has been suggested for each resource, you should evaluate the maturity of your child and select the resource best suited for him or her. Keep in mind their physical, emotional, social, mental, and spiritual growth. A parent may choose to start his eleven-year-old son with the middle-aged children's book, *My Body and Me*, instead of the preadolescent book, *Sex! What's That?*, because of the child's level of maturity. A parent with a mature nine-year-old daughter may choose the preadolescent book instead of the book for middle-aged children because of her level of maturity and the situations she may be facing.

The ideal process is to begin when our children are young, using each book at the appropriate time during their development. You know your child and, after careful consideration, should be able to select the resource best suited for him or her.

What Do I Do After I Select a Resource?

Acquaint yourself with the materials, both the parent's material in this book and the book for your child.

Let your child or youth know that you are going through these materials and that you want to go over them with him or her.

When you are familiar with the material, begin by setting aside time to go through them with your child. In the case of an older child or youth, give the materials to her to begin reading.

With the smaller child, begin reading and going through the material together in short periods of time according to her attention span.

When our children were small, we found the best time was in the evening as a part of our "getting ready for bed" ritual.

With an older child or youth, set a time that the two of you can discuss what he has been reading. Be ready for him not to ask any questions. Therefore, have some questions ready without invading his privacy.

Should fathers do this with sons and mothers with daughters? When our children were small, both of us talked with our children about sexual matters. As they have grown older, it has been more male to male and female to female, but the important thing is that it gets done. Some of the things faced uniquely by boys and girls are addressed by the materials so that either father or mother can cover this information.

Keep the books available so that children can refer to them when they have a question that they may feel embarrassed about asking directly.

How Do I Talk With My Child?

Here are some guidelines that I have found important over the years in regard to my conversations with our children about sexual matters:

1. Be ready for silence from your child.

2. If you are asked about a term or some information that you do not know about, show the child how to find it in these resources, or in others, or do some research yourself so that the question does not remain unanswered.

3. Be willing to say, "I don't know, but we'll find the answer."

4. Do not shame a child for asking an honest question.

5. Appropriately show your own humanity or struggles with your sexual development without sharing what would be hard for the child to handle.

6. Be prepared to answer questions that the child may have about "school yard" or curse words.

7. Recognize the feelings of the child in regard to his or her difficulty in talking about these matters, or shame they may feel, or the feeling that they should know something that they do not.

8. Be ready to anticipate questions they may be afraid to ask.

9. Be aware of some of the myths they may have heard about such things as breast development, menstruation, "wet dreams," masturbation, kissing, petting, getting pregnant, AIDS, etc.

10. Keep in mind their physical, emotional, social, mental, and spiritual growth.

Parents and Church Leaders Working Together

Christian sex education in your church may consist of a one-time training and orientation session to introduce parents to the resources in the series. It may go beyond that to include using the materials for preadolescents and adolescents in a supplemental group study at the church to support what parents are doing in the home.

Whatever it involves, how do you move from someone having a conviction about your church providing help on Christian sex education to making it a reality? The key issue is getting the parents and church leaders unified in their support of providing this help. To do that, the key person taking the initiative must have in mind and be ready to name the major needs for this effort and be ready to deal with the major objections that may be raised. The information in this resource is crucial in that regard.

Assume you are a layperson wanting to start this program in your church. Who are the key persons in your church whom you believe would share your enthusiasm? Begin talking with them about it. Share some of the materials with them. If they concur, let your pastor or a church staff member know of your interest and your willingness to work on this.

As a pastor, it would be important to me when you presented this to me and/or another church staff member that you are prepared to cover the following.

• Be clear that this is not just one more thing you are adding to my "to do" list.

• Let me know that you are seeking my support, and that there are laypeople who are ready to work on this.

• Be ready to show how this program can relate to the growth of the church and meet the needs of families in the community.

• Be prepared to address any questions and concerns. How will families in the community be invited to the church to gain help with a need most parents have but are not sure how to meet? How can we meet the needs of two sets of parents: those who want their children to be involved in a Christian sex education group and those who don't? How can this program help people in the community see that the church is concerned for families?

• Have men as well as women involved in presenting this to me and/or other staff members.

• Assuming staff support, ask for suggestions on next steps for getting this started.

• Let's pray together about this effort.

If the pastor or a staff member, with the support of the pastor, is seeking to begin this ministry, calling together some key leaders for a meeting may be the first step. This meeting could include the family enrichment committee if there is one, youth and children's workers, some interested parents, and possibly the chairman of deacons. In this meeting, use the following agenda.

First Meeting
    1. The need for such a ministry.
    2. A clear statement of the objectives of this program.
    3. Address some of the major objections that may be raised.

> **Churches Supporting Parents**
>
> 1. Initial presentation of Christian Sex Education program to parents
> 2. Church approval to provide the program of Christian Sex Education
> 3. Church orienting parents to provide Christian sex education in the home
> 4. Parents using the resources in the home with their children and youth
> 5. Parent support groups organized through the church (optional)
> 6. Supplementary sessions at church for preadolescents and/or adolescents (parental permission recommended)

4. Overview the materials.
5. Discuss initial suggestions on implementation.
6. Distribute some of the materials to each of the participants.
7. Set the date for another meeting of the group. Give each person time to review the material.
8. Pray together for the children and youth as well as their parents.

The agenda for the next meeting of this group should include the following elements.

Second Meeting
1. Response and questions about the material.
2. A call for commitment to this ministry.
3. A time of brainstorming how each person can build support and enthusiasm for this effort as it is formally presented to the church.
4. Ways each person present is willing to work in this ministry once it is approved and started.
5. Suggestions and specific assignments about next steps related to approval.
6. A prayer of commitment.

In the next section, we will deal with implementation strategies beginning with the formal steps of church approval.

Clear communication is probably the most important thing in keeping parents and church leaders working together well. This communication also builds continued support for such a ministry. Progress reports to the staff, to parents, and to the church are important. Periodic updating and evaluation meetings keep things on track and keep key people informed and supportive.

I am helped tremendously as a pastor when I hear from people about how a ministry of our church has helped them or someone else. These reports help maintain my support, give me good information to pass on to other church leaders to maintain their support, and provide me with an opportunity to pass on a specific compliment and word of appreciation to the persons leading in this ministry.

Also, I am helped by specific suggestions from persons involved in ministries about ways I can continue to support a ministry. For instance, a word of announcement or appreciation from the pulpit may be needed. A column in the church newsletter may be important, or recognition of a particular individual's efforts. Also, I may need to lead one of the sessions or just show up for it with a word of encouragement. Lay leaders in our church help me tremendously when they let me know these things.

Planning, Implementing, and Evaluating Christian Sex Education in Your Church

Planning

Assuming the basic step has been taken to build support for this effort, the specific task of seeking church approval is needed. Even so, further planning precedes this task. Here are some suggested steps in planning.

1. Determine who will develop the strategy for implementing the program. The family enrichment committee is the logical group to develop this. If there is not such a committee, it may be an ad hoc group involving parents, church leaders, and staff.

2. Define the objectives. See the objectives as described in the Preface of this book.

3. Develop responses to anticipated questions or objections.

4. Determine the target group for initial efforts. This may be all parents in the church, or you may decide to begin with parents of young children or another group of parents. (Your church may also choose to offer a supplemental group study for preadolescents and adolescents to support what parents are doing in the home. If so, consider conducting a preliminary class for parents, maybe after the orientation session, to review the material that will be used in the supplemental group sessions. For suggestions about sessions for parents, see the chapter, "Training Parents in Providing Christian Sex Education." For suggestions about sessions for preadolescents and adolescents, see "Supplementary Group Study for Preadolescents and Adolescents.")

5. Outline the plan that will be presented and when it will be scheduled. This should include the initial parent orientation session (found later in this book) as well as any supplemental group study sessions offered. Also consider parent support group meetings during the process as a help to those parents who might seek the encouragement of others.

6. Determine budget impact and/or cost to participants. Be sure to fac-

tor in the costs of outside advertising if the community is to be invited, although that may not be done until after a first run of the program.

7. Decide on which person or persons will present this to the decision-making group in the church and then to the congregation in a business meeting.

8. Determine what materials will be needed in the way of handouts or overhead transparencies when it is presented to the church.

9. Develop initial suggestions about who will lead the session(s).

10. Pray together for a successful presentation to the church that will lead to acceptance and build support for this effort.

11. Go through the steps necessary for church approval.

Implementation

1. Begin to select, enlist, and train the workers needed for implementation, working with the appropriate committee in the church.

2. After finalizing the suggested schedule, work with the staff to see if there are any conflicts and to schedule it on the church calendar. In regard to scheduling, it is wise to confer with the parents who may be involved so that times are selected that will attract as many of the target group as possible.

3. With projected attendance estimated, order materials from the Customer Service Center (1-800-458-2772) or through a local Christian book store.

4. Develop a publicity plan including mailouts, church newsletter, posters, flyers, notices in the Sunday bulletin, and announcements in church meetings including worship services and Sunday School. For printed materials, enlist the help of persons who can design graphics to make the material attractive.

5. Develop a registration plan for parents to sign up in advance for the initial orientation session. This will aid in planning and get persons committed to attending.

6. Arrange for the facilities, including the room, the arrangement of the room, and materials and equipment needed.

7. Develop an evaluation process and share with leaders/teachers. See the next section.

8. Arrange for childcare for parents that will be attending.

9. Work with the appropriate people in your church to ensure that the room is unlocked and that heating/cooling is adjusted.

10. Have signs directing persons from the entrance of the building to the room where the initial orientation session is being held.

11. Enlist persons to greet people, get them a name tag, pass out materials, and be ready to assist the group leader. Enlist parents from the target group to do this.

12. Work with the church office staff to copy any materials that will be needed as handouts, and provide materials and equipment as requested.

13. A week before the initial orientation session, send out reminder cards to all persons registered.

14. Check room arrangement, equipment, and materials on the day of the session.

15. Conduct the initial orientation session.

Evaluation

1. Using the objectives of the program, develop an evaluation form to be filled out by the participants. Include the following on the form.

• The statement of the major objectives with a response indicating how well the participants felt these objectives were reached using a numerical scale of one to five or a word scale from excellent to poor.

• A rating scale on the material used.

• Space for each participant to respond to the question, "What were the three most helpful things for you in this session?"

• Space for each participant to respond to the question, "What suggestions would you recommend as this program is presented in the future?"

• Space for any general comments.

2. Develop an evaluation form to be completed by the leaders and teachers responsible for the sessions. They should evaluate:

• the planning, implementation, and evaluation process;
• the materials used;
• the facilities;
• the equipment; and,
• suggestions for future development of the program.

3. Conduct a meeting of the participants six months after the completion of the program to evaluate it after further implementation in the home. The questions on the evaluation can be used as the agenda.

All of the details outlined above are important in reaching the goal of helping children and youth have healthy concepts of themselves as created by God with the gift of sexuality. Through these efforts, these children and youth will be equipped with good information and with values centered in their Christian faith. Decisions can be made and conviction stated on the basis of what God teaches us about how we are to be responsible and joyful stewards of all He has given us, including our sexuality.

You, as a parent and/or leader in this effort, have embarked on an important and crucial task. Commit this task to the Lord in prayer, and He will reward your efforts.

Parents Providing Christian Sex Education

Biblical Foundations for Sex Education

Michael Fink

When Proverbs 22:6 admonishes us to "Train up a child in the way he should go," it states God's intention for us in educating our children. This verse also states part of our divine commission as parents and workers with children. Three aspects of this proverb deserve our attention as we begin our consideration of the biblical foundations for Christian sex education.

The Purpose

First, let's note the *purpose* of our educational task implied in the word "train." The biblical word that has been translated "train" is found only five times in the Old Testament. In Hebrew the word is *chanak*, a word related to Hanukkah, the Jewish Feast of Dedication that celebrates the rededication of the Jerusalem temple in 164 B.C. Thus, *training a child is related to the idea of dedicating the child to God and to God's purposes.* Training involves entrusting the child to God with the prayer that God will bring devotion and dedication out of our instruction and discipline.

Dedicating a child recognizes the importance of the human will in teaching. Training is not squeezing a person into a preset mold. Rather, training invokes the heart, appeals to the will, and invites commitment. We acknowledge the role of the Holy Spirit in convicting of sin and renewing the heart. Training is not indoctrination but regeneration; it is not reforming but transforming; it does not produce conformity, but reflects genuine holiness.

None of this transpires without the presence and power of God. We do not bring about Christian moral development in the life of another. Rather we work as agents with God for the communicating of His truth. We entrust the ones under our care into God's care. That is why training is dedicating or devoting the child.

The Scope

The *scope* of training is implied in the words "in the way he should go." A literal translation of this expression would be "according to his way" and would recognize "way" in terms of the child's conduct. Two conclusions can be drawn from these words.

1. Dedicating a child to a way involves some standards of conduct. That is why translators have interpreted this phrase "the way he *should* go." We might speak of these standards in terms of good and bad behavior or right and wrong conduct. Who determines these? Ultimately the way the child should go is defined by the teachings of the Bible, not society. The direction toward which we dedicate the child is for him to do God's will. The Bible establishes the standard by which all conduct, both personal and corporate, is to be measured.

2. The phrase "according to his way" is based on the recognition that the word "his" most certainly refers to the child. Training a child according to the child's way is a recognition of the uniqueness and particular needs of each child. Far too much of our training is an attempt to secure social conformity rather than to nurture the unique gift that is within each child. While holding to the Bible as the fixed standard by which all conduct is to be measured, we dedicate the child in accordance with his unique needs, interests, and abilities rather than imposing on him every fixed expression of social conformity.

The Principle

There is a *principle* that comes with our commission to dedicate a child according to his way. Proverbs 22:6 continues, "and when he is old, he will not depart from it." Some have tried to claim that principle when their approach to training has more resembled breaking the will than dedicating the child. Others have forced upon the child "the way *I think* he should go." Neither approach will embody the principle. The principle is demonstrated as we entrust the child to God, guide the child in discovering and applying the teachings of the Bible, and nurture the child's unique gifts and abilities.

Equally important is to recognize that the principle is dependent on the will of the child. God does not customarily override the human will in order to ensure that one of His truths is fulfilled. Even when parents dedicate a child according to His way, the power and influence of Satan is at work. At some point the child must personally choose God's way, and even the best intentioned parents cannot produce such commitment automatically.

If dedicating a child is an act of faith and trust in God, can we not also trust God's principle? The principle says we can trust God to bring to fruitfulness the seeds of faith we have sown in a child's life. When a child is dedicated to the Lord, nurtured in a family of faith, exposed to committed believers, strengthened in the fellowship of a faithful church, and guided in the principles of God's Word, we can trust God to bring this principle to fruition by the power of His Spirit.

Basis in the Scriptures

Most of us will grant the need to train up a child in the way he should go, but we may feel quite uncomfortable thinking about "the way he should go" including Christian sex education. Yet, if we believe the Bible is the scope of our Christian training, we will have to acknowledge that the concern for sexual morality is an important part of the Bible's teachings. Think for a moment about what the Bible reveals concerning God's intentions for persons, for marriage, and for families. Sexuality is part of each of these.

Most of us will recall that one of the Ten Commandments deals with adultery, but we may have overlooked the fact that scores of other Old Testament laws speak of God's concern for sexual purity, marital fidelity, and family solidarity. These concerns underscore the need for biblically-based, Christian sex education.

Sexual immorality has threatened God's people in every generation. From the perverted practices in Sodom and Gomorrah, to the sensual worship of Baal among the Canaanites, to the orgiastic observances in the temple of Aphrodite in Corinth, to the "Jezebel" who enticed the church in Thyatira to immorality, the Bible records the struggle of God's people against sexual sin. These things were "written for our instruction, that through perseverance and the encouragement of the Scriptures we might have hope" (Rom. 15:4, NASB).

Add to these the numerous pivotal events in the Bible that have sexual implications (for example, David and Bathsheba), the celebration of sexual intimacy in the Song of Songs, and the frequent comparison of unfaithfulness to God with that of marital unfaithfulness. When the whole biblical record is in view, we immediately begin to see that human sexuality is a recurring reality on the pages of the Bible.

From these images, laws, teachings, and examples, we shall attempt to lift up the biblical ethic and the implications that ethic has for Christian sex education.

Reflections of God's Intent

As is true with many significant biblical themes, our examination must begin with Genesis. In creation, we discover many important reflections of God's intention for humanity.

Be Fruitful
From the creation on the third day of plants yielding seed and trees bearing fruit (see Gen. 1:11), through the creation of aquatic animals and birds on the fifth day (see Gen. 1:20-21), to the creation of land animals and finally man on the sixth day (see Gen. 1:24-27), God's work was centered in a concern that His creatures "be fruitful and increase in number; fill the earth" (see Gen. 1:28, NIV). Indeed, God's first com-

mand for reproduction of the species was given on the fifth day, even before land animals and man had been created (see Gen. 1:22). The command was repeated on the sixth day (see Gen. 1:28).

Humankind shares in this command with all other parts of God's living creation. We also share in God's assessment that His creation was "good" (see Gen. 1:4,10,12,18,21,25). Indeed, after the creation of man, "God saw all that he had made, and it was very good" (see Gen. 1:31, NIV). God's plan for human reproduction should be cherished as a reflection of His original intent.

The Image of God

Humanity, however, is not merely another animal in God's creative design. The Bible records that God set persons apart from the rest of His creation by creating "man in his own image" (Gen. 1:27). While volumes have been written trying to describe exactly what that image of God is, the Bible gives only hints of what it means. The introduction of plural pronouns in Genesis 1:26 certainly says that the capacity for relationship is part of the divine image in us—a relationship with God and relationships with one another. The use of the words "rule" (Gen. 1:26,28, NIV) and "subdue" (Gen. 1:28, NIV) speak to the capacity for personal initiative and activity. What we see in other parts of this chapter—God's creative activity, His orderly work, His categorizing and naming, His assessment of value, and His careful provision for His creatures' needs—reflect something of His nature, His image, in which humanity shares. As persons bearing the image of God, we have unique, significant, and eternal value. Our relationships, activity, work, and living must reflect that divine image.

Another significant point is found in the statement, "in the image of God he created him; male and female he created them" (Gen. 1:27, NIV). God's image and likeness encompasses both sexes fully. Neither maleness nor femaleness can claim exclusive likeness to God. Sexuality is something we share in common with our fellow creatures, not something we possess from bearing the divine image (compare Matt. 22:30). Yet, God created us male and female. Sexuality is part of God's gift of life. When we express our sexuality, we do so, not as mere animals, but as image-of-God creatures sharing in God's gift of life and enjoying our capacity for intimate relationship.

A Suitable Helper

Genesis 2 gives us fuller insight into God's purpose in creating man male and female. The first thing God discovered about His creation that was "not good" was that Adam was "alone" (Gen. 2:18). A creature endowed with the capacity for living in relationship requires an appropriate companion.

Of all the other living creatures God had made, none was found to be "suitable" as a companion for Adam. The Hebrew word translated "suitable" (Gen. 2:20, NIV) literally means "according to what is in front of." In more current terms we would say "corresponding to" or "equal and adequate to." The companionship that fulfills the capacity for intimate human relationship is found in a partner—not in an object or a pet or an inferior being.

The term translated "helper" also is suggestive of God's divine intent in creation. The Hebrew term means both "help" and "succor" (something that furnishes relief). Human aloneness ultimately finds its relief in one who so corresponds to man that she can be said to be "bone of my bones and flesh of my flesh" (Gen. 2:23, NIV).

One Flesh

Ultimately the companionship between male and female finds expression in an intimate union that the Bible calls "one flesh" (Gen. 2:24). That union is first of all a physical union that results from sexual intercourse. The apostle Paul commented on this physical union when he wrote, "Do you not know that he who unites himself with a prostitute is one with her in body? For it is said, 'The two will become one flesh' " (1 Cor. 6:16, NIV).

Too often today, persons view sexual intercourse as a temporary encounter between persons without any binding of spirit or bonding of personality. The Bible teaches that this is not so. Sexual intercourse cannot be engaged in by two physical bodies and maintain their distinct separateness. But more transpires in intercourse than the physical joining. With the sexual bonding comes a deeper, emotional, psychic bond that can be denied but cannot be ignored without great harm to the persons involved. The repeated joining and rending of one flesh damages the capacity for fulfilling intimate relationship and destroys the divine purpose for male-female companionship.

As circumcision was to Abraham an outward symbol of the covenant and baptism is to us a symbol of obedience, repentance, faith, and regeneration, so is one flesh an outward symbol of a spiritual reality. God intended for sexual intercourse to encompass both a leaving and a cleaving (Gen. 2:24). While Genesis speaks only of a man leaving his father and mother, the rest of Scripture is clear that one flesh involves both the man and the woman forsaking all others. Sexual intercourse produces one flesh, and one flesh is intended by God to involve an exclusive and permanent commitment of one man and one woman to each other.

Thus, God's original purpose is expressed in His creating us as sexual beings intended to reflect God's image and live in right relationships with others. Our sexuality is intended to be expressed in the faithful and committed relationship of one man and one woman bound together as one flesh. Christian sex education must affirm the goodness of God's creative purpose. It must emphasize God's intention for persons to live in relationship. And it must uphold God's plan for sexual expression only in the committed and permanent relationship of marriage.

Consequences of the Fall

Chapter 2 of Genesis concludes, "The man and his wife were both naked, and they felt no shame (NIV)." Adam and Eve originally fulfilled God's purpose in creation. They lived in intimate companionship without shame, embarrassment, guilt, or fear.

Sin changed all of that. When Adam and Eve disobeyed God and ate the fruit of "the tree of the knowledge of good and evil" (Gen. 2:17), they forsook God's intentions and purposes for them. The consequences of that sin (disobedience) affected them and their relationships.

Opened Eyes

The serpent told Eve that eating the fruit would open her eyes (see Gen. 3:5). That proved to be so (see Gen. 3:7), but the opened eyes altered Adam and Eve's perception of themselves and their relationship. First, they realized that they were naked. Then they covered themselves. Their original companionship, which had been without shame, embarrassment, guilt, or fear, was replaced by self-conscious embarrassment. Their openness was replaced by protectiveness. Their peace became fear (see Gen. 3:10). Their one-flesh intimacy deteriorated into self-centered blaming that set one against the other (see Gen. 3:12-13). Their closeness with God turned to hiding from Him (see Gen. 3:8,10).

This distortion of God's original intent that results from sin affects all of us. Our hopes for companionship, intimacy, and freedom frequently are dashed by protectiveness, self-centeredness, fear, and shame. Our relationships are characterized by one sinner relating to another. As a result, we all fall short of the high ideal God intended for us.

Like God

The serpent also told Eve that eating the fruit would let her "be like God" (Gen. 3:5, NIV). The irony of this statement is that Eve and Adam already were image-of-God creatures. They were like God in more ways than any other part of the created order. Their desire to be like God and their decision to disobey God reveal that the temptation for Adam and Eve was to *be* God, not merely to be like Him.

The refusal to live under the sovereign lordship of God continues as the root problem of our lives. Disobeying God, rejecting His will, and refusing to accept His purpose for us lead to emptiness, pain, suffering, and eventually eternal separation from God.

Knowing Good and Evil

We can infer from the Scriptures that until Adam and Eve's disobedience, they had only known good. God's assessment that all of His creation was "very good" (Gen. 1:31) implies that Adam and Eve's initial experience with life was with its goodness. In disobeying God and eating the forbidden fruit, they came to know evil.

We cannot fully understand what knowing evil means when applied to God (see Gen. 3:5,22). Whatever it means, it surely does not mean that God shares in evil or becomes evil. We can understand what knowing evil means when applied to humanity. The curse of sin that brings enmity (see Gen 3:15), pain (see Gen. 3:16), unfulfilled desire (see Gen. 3:16), hierarchical relationships (see Gen. 3:16), painful toil (see Gen. 3:17), and death (see Gen. 3:19) are realities with which we are well acquainted.

The Hebrew word translated "knowing" in verses 5 and 22 and "realized" in verse 7 (NIV) has the meaning of intimate knowledge and personal experience. It is the same word used in Genesis 4:1 to speak of sexual relations ("Adam knew Eve"). The result of sin was that Adam, Eve, and all of their descendants became intimately acquainted with and personally experienced in evil. Note that in Genesis 5:3, Adam's son was born in his image and likeness (including the sinful nature). All the good that God had intended can now be experienced as evil also. Lust can be disguised as love. Sexual intimacy can be exploited. Freedom can become license. Trust can be abused. All that God intended people to be in relationship with Him and with each other now can be experienced as its opposite.

Scope of Concern

The whole realm of human sexuality now lives in this tension between good and evil. Good in its creation and wholesome in its divine intent, sex can be distorted and degraded into evil. Genesis reveals in only a few chapters how complete this distortion became.

• "The Lord saw how great man's wickedness on the earth had become, and that every inclination of the thoughts of his heart was only evil all the time. The Lord was grieved that he had made man on the earth, and his heart was filled with pain" (Gen. 6:5-6, NIV).

• "The earth was corrupt in God's sight and was full of violence. God saw how corrupt the earth had become, for all the people on earth had corrupted their ways" (Gen. 6:11-12, NIV).

• "Every inclination of his heart is evil from childhood" (Gen. 8:21, NIV).

God's response to humanity's corruption was to begin again. He destroyed the earth by flood (see Gen. 6:9—8:18) and established a covenant with Noah and his sons (see Gen. 9:1-17). That covenant stipulated a respect for life symbolized in the prohibition against eating meat that still contained its blood (Gen. 9:4).

Since Noah was the father of all humanity (the church seems to have reasoned), the stipulations of God's covenant with him apply to all people. The requirements of circumcision and ritual purity, which were part of the covenants with Abraham and Moses, were not placed on Gentiles. The church's decision preserved the central roles of grace and faith in salvation (see Acts 15:9,11).

From a biblical perspective, sexual morality is an expectation of God for all humanity. Surely in our day when abortion, child pornography, promiscuity, and sexually transmitted diseases like AIDS have such broad social implications, we cannot ignore God's injunction that persons abstain from sexual immorality. As we focus on basic societal issues related to the respect for life, all aspects of sexual abuse and perversion must be addressed.

Lessons from the Law

While the early church decided not to burden Gentiles with all the requirements contained in the law of Moses, it certainly did not intend to ignore these important teachings. The law of Moses continued to be "preached in every city" and "read in the synagogues on every Sabbath" (Acts 15:21, NIV).

Some in the early church, however, tried to cast off the law as if it had no relevance at all. These persons perhaps based their views on a distortion of some of Paul's teachings (see Gal. 3:10-14; Rom. 7:6; 10:4; compare 2 Pet. 3:16). But the consistent view conveyed in the New Testament is that the law reflects God's divine will. Matthew 5:17-20 and Luke 16:16-17 certainly give Jesus' fulfillment of the law, and passages such as Romans 7:12,14; 8:4 give Paul's affirmation of the law's importance.

Torah

The fundamental meaning of "law" may help us understand more fully its role. The Hebrew word translated "law" is *torah*. This word means "teaching," "instruction," "direction," or "revelation." Far from implying a narrow, capricious, legalistic set of restrictions, the term instead conveys the idea of divine guidance that points the way to fulfilling life.

Our teaching in Christian sex education also must be *torah*. Children and youth need guidance that will point them toward a fulfilling life. A narrow, capricious, and legalistic application of moral law may achieve temporary conformity to our standards, but it often fails to capture the heart.

Covenant

The Old Testament law was given in the context of developing a covenant relationship. God took the initiative in calling a people unto Himself and establishing a covenant with them. The covenants established with Abraham and Moses became the binding promises between God and His chosen people, Israel. The purpose of the covenants was to bless the people and to enable the people to bless others (see Gen. 12; 17).

Christian sex education can have a dimension of covenant too. Ideally, families are covenant communities bound together by blessing and being blessed. So are churches. When based on commitment to God

27

and one another, our families and churches provide a context in which Christian moral values are developed and nurtured.

Benefit

Jesus established a principle in understanding the law that is applicable here. In dealing with controversy over the application of the Sabbath laws, Jesus stated, "The Sabbath was made for man, not man for the Sabbath" (Mark 2:27, NIV). The fundamental purpose of the law was to benefit persons, not to force them into subservience of abstract moral principles. As "Lord of the Sabbath," Jesus rejected the petty rules and regulations of the scribes and Pharisees. He focused instead on internal issues of the heart (Matt. 5:21-48) and weightier matters of the law (Matt. 23:23). He summarized the whole law in terms of love of God and love of others (Matt. 22:37-40).

What a marked contrast to the way we often approach Christian moral development! Rather than legalistic rules forced on the child in order to prevent embarrassment caused by the child's misbehavior, the law becomes moral guidance based on covenant and love. It is designed to bless and benefit, to point toward a fulfilling life. By example and by instruction, the meaning of the law is taught. Through love of God and love of the child, the application of the law is sought. In the supportive community of family and church, the essence of the law is caught. Thus "We know that the law is good if one uses it properly" (1 Tim. 1:8, NIV).

Barriers of Protection

The law is not merely to prohibit or restrict; it is to provide God's way for human fulfillment and happiness. The law protects from all of those forces, influences, and experiences that would inhibit our growing and living as God's people. Observing the law will not bring salvation; failure to observe it will bring pain, suffering, alienation, and even death.

What, then, are the purposes of the Old Testament laws related to human sexuality?

Protection of Marriage

One of the chief and most obvious purposes of the law is to protect the sacred commitments involved in the marriage relationship. The Bible clearly teaches that marriage is a God-ordained relationship intended to join one man and one woman in an exclusive and permanent union. While many experiences related to marriage are cultural and vary from society to society, one thread must run through them all if we are to experience all that God intends. God intends for marriages to be characterized by fidelity and permanence. The Ten Commandments reflect this concern in the direct statement, "You shall not commit adultery" (Ex. 20:14).

Sexual infidelity is the obvious object of this commandment. But

Jesus clearly taught that sexual infidelity comes from the heart (see Mark 7:21-23). Sexual fidelity is of great importance in marriage. Commitment, communication, kindness, unselfish love, and a host of other spiritual traits are also important. The spiritual traits often are neglected long before sexual infidelity arises. When the spiritual traits are nurtured, sexual faithfulness can be easily preserved.

Sexual fidelity cannot be taught merely with words; it also must be taught by practice and example. Children and youth will respond positively to the fidelity they see each day in the attention, affection, kindness, and concern expressed between their parents and between other marriage partners.

The casual attitude toward sexual fidelity exhibited by so many in our society produces mistrust, emptiness, disillusionment, and ultimately, shattered relationships. God wants to protect us from those consequences and has given us His commandments to guide us. Obedience to His commands serves to preserve and protect marriages.

Protection of Family and Children

Many Old Testament laws are designed to preserve family integrity and to protect children from exploitation. Leviticus 18:6-18 is an example of such divine concern. This passage details the multiple relations of family that must be protected from sexual abuse and exploitation. The immediate context of the passage reveals God's concern that His people be holy as He is holy and avoid the sexual abuses of their pagan neighbors (Lev. 18:3; 19:2). Those are important concerns that are worthy of our focused attention. We also know today much about the personal and family devastation that results from incest, sexual abuse, and sexual exploitation.

The Hebrew expression used throughout the Leviticus passage literally means "do not uncover the nakedness of." This reminds us that in the natural intimacy of family relationships, parents must carefully develop a proper understanding of modesty, privacy, and propriety. Part of Christian sex education is developing a respect for one's body as a good gift from God while at the same time discovering how God intends for the body to function, to be handled, and to be related to others. "Covering nakedness" is part of equipping the child to appreciate and value the personal, private, sacred, and intimate aspects of the body.

Parents and other adults have the power to bless or destroy children by the manner in which they relate to themselves, their mates, and their children as sexual beings. God has given parents the responsibility of protecting the child from sexual abuse and exploitation. Parents must prepare children from potentially abusive situations they may encounter outside the home. Parents must accept the role of evaluating and controlling media influences that come into the home. Parents also must uphold the biblical ideals of chastity before marriage and fidelity afterwards. God's laws guide us in protecting the integrity of the family and the well-being of the child.

Protection of Community

The concern for sexual morality in the Ten Commandments goes beyond the issue of adultery and the protection of the integrity of marriage relationships. Adultery also affects relationships between neighbors and can strain the bonds of social and community life. The Tenth Commandment addresses the sin of covetousness and explicitly warns against coveting "your neighbor's wife." Persons who live in the interdependent relationships of church and community can destroy the fabric of their society by engaging in promiscuous and adulterous relationships.

Paul pointed out that the Tenth Commandment was a commandment that convicted the heart of sin (see Rom. 7:7-25). Breaking the command destroys the central barrier that deters adultery and other sexual sins. Old Testament prohibitions against covetousness and New Testament teachings about lust seek to build a barrier against the dehumanizing results of these sins. God intends for persons to relate to their neighbors in what has been called an *I-Thou* relationship. We relate to them as persons like ourselves. We act toward them in the fashion as we would want them to act toward us. Covetousness and lust are *I-It* sins. When we relate to others as objects to be desired or crave them as bodies to be possessed, we dehumanize them and destroy the possibility of community.

At many other points the Old Testament law reflects the community's concern for prohibiting those kinds of behavior that cause distrust and alienation within the community. Exodus 22:16-17, for example, deals with the seduction of a virgin and tells how the families involved were to resolve the concern. Not only does this legal prescription communicate the seriousness of the offense for the families involved, it also points to the bonding that results from sexual intercourse. The one who had been seduced as a virgin was bound to the seducer and was to become his wife unless her father absolutely refused to give her to the man. By prohibiting sexual intercourse without an accompanying commitment, the community guarded the relationships between neighbors.

In the same context in which we saw God's concern for protecting the integrity of families, we also find a prohibition against uncovering the nakedness of your neighbor's wife (see Lev. 18:20). Intimacy is intended as an exclusive dynamic between husband and wife. When a person engages in personal and sexual intimacy with someone other than spouse, the person is "defiled." Defilement is the biblical way of speaking of a person who has engaged in behavior that displeases God. The failure to reflect God's holy character in our relationships displeases God.

Engaging in personal and sexual intimacy outside of marriage undermines the trust that is so basic to the marriage relationship. It also undermines the trust between neighbors on which community is built. God's law protects us from the enmity and alienation that sexual immorality brings to community life.

Protection of Personal Integrity

The human mind has been able to devise many corrupt ways of expressing human sexuality. Many contemporary distortions of sex have been magnified by television, movies, and videos. The restraints placed on these practices in the close-knit societies of yesterday have broken down. Our world needs biblical guidelines that will promote human well-being in the face of sexual license.

The Bible directly prohibits some sexual deviations and provides principles that can be applied to all. Some have argued from the relative silence of the Bible on many sexual matters. Their principle seems to be that if the Bible doesn't explicitly prohibit a practice, Christian freedom will allow you to do as you please. Others try to explain away biblical laws by saying the laws reflect the limited views of an ancient culture. Much of the discussion reflects a contemporary obsession with all things sexual.

Homosexual activity and sexual acts with animals are two practices explicitly prohibited in the Old Testament law (see Ex. 22:19; Lev. 18:22-23; 20:13,15-16; Deut. 27:21). Prostitution practiced in conjunction with pagan worship was considered detestable (see Deut. 23:17-18; 1 Kings 14:24; 15:12; 22:46; 2 Kings 23:7), but laws also restricted other kinds of prostitution (see Lev. 19:29; 21:7,9,14; Deut. 22:21). Rape (Deut. 22:25,28) and sexual violence (see Gen. 19:1-10; compare Judg. 19) are condemned as well. While full treatment of these and other sexual deviations would be impossible in this context, we can draw some principles that reflect God's concern for persons and their integrity.

1. The Bible consistently emphasizes purity or chastity prior to marriage. The Bible views sexual intercourse as a bonding of two persons that should occur only in marriage and clearly teaches the importance of restricting sexual intercourse to the marriage relationship.

2. The biblical teachings emphasize sexual relationships characterized by exclusive commitment and faithfulness. Promiscuity and infidelity are forbidden.

3. The Bible condemns what Paul was later to call "unnatural" relations (Rom. 1:26-27, NIV). Sexual relations other than those between one man and one woman were deemed to be "unnatural."

4. The Bible emphasizes the goodness of the natural sexual relation between husband and wife. In 1 Corinthians 7:3-5, Paul stressed the mutuality of sexual relations within marriage. Sexual expression is a normal and natural part of being married. Notice that this passage says nothing about procreation, sexual intercourse that results in the birth of a child. This shows that sexual relations within marriage express the one-flesh union even when procreation is not the purpose or outcome. The principles of mutuality emphasize the mutual benefit of husband and wife and exclude any expression not mutually agreeable to both.

Sexual practices must focus on and support the bonding quality in the relationship. Coercion, force, violence, or compulsion have no place in sexual relationships. Focus on individual or personal sensation and pleasure to the exclusion of mutuality also detracts from the divine purpose for sex. Sexual intercourse is meant to be good and should be enjoyable and pleasurable, but enjoyment must not be at the expense of the marriage partner and the sense of union sex is intended to promote.

We have summarized this section under the heading "protection of personal integrity." That emphasis, properly understood, brings together the biblical teachings related to deviant sexual practices. God's concern is that sexuality promote personal integrity, not demean it. Sex is good and was designed by God as a means of expressing human wholeness. Neither partner in a sexual relationship should ever experience dehumanization to the point of one partner being used as an object of pleasure for the other. The sense of integrity that grows out of sexual intercourse should first of all be one that fulfills the wholeness of each individual in the relationship. A sense of being loved and of having worth should result. Beyond that, the two partners also should experience the wholeness of the two being one. Any sexual expression should promote unity, mutuality, and oneness of purpose and hope.

Resources for Renewal

We have given extensive attention to Old Testament teachings on human sexuality because they provide the foundation for the New Testament. The Old Testament ethic was not eclipsed in the New Testament, but neither was it found to be fully adequate for dealing with human sin. Even in the latter stages of the Old Testament, prophetic voices began to recognize that a covenant engraved on stone could not overcome mankind's inclination toward sin. What was needed was a covenant engraved on human hearts (see Jer. 31:31-34).

A New Heart
Ezekiel envisioned the new heart that was required for God's people to live in keeping with God's expectations (see Ezek. 11:19; 18:31; 36:26), and he recognized that such a heart could only come as something God would "give." The gift of grace for which Ezekiel longed has been made possible through what God did in His Son, Jesus Christ. As Christians, we speak of the results of this gift as conversion, regeneration, and new birth. All of these New Testament images reflect an action taken at the initiative of God and in cooperation with human faith. Through the power of His Spirit, God sets aside a people for Himself, calls them to trust Him as their Lord and Savior, and transforms them into a holy people dedicated to doing His will in the world.
Christian sex education cannot be complete without this recognition

of mankind's need for redemption. No one by sheer moral strength is able to obey God's commands. No one can know the complete, fulfilling life that God desires for us without acknowledging sin, confessing it to God, repenting of that sin, and accepting God's forgiveness made possible through the life, death, and resurrection of Jesus. So complete is this experience of salvation that Paul wrote, "If anyone is in Christ, he is a new creation" (2 Cor. 5:17, NIV). Ultimately Christian moral development is an inward-outward experience. God transforms our hearts, gives us a new affection, and instills within us a desire to do His will.

A High Ideal

The new heart we receive in salvation does not automatically translate into a life that perfectly reflects God's will. Paul struggled with the tension between the good he wanted to do and the evil he kept on doing (see Rom. 7:14-25), and so will every Christian. Paul found his inner being waging war with his sinful nature. He knew the final victory had been won through Jesus Christ our Lord, but he knew he must battle every day with his sinful nature.

Recognizing this battle within us must not deter us, however, from striving for the high ideal that Jesus established for His disciples: "Be perfect, therefore, as your heavenly Father is perfect" (Matt. 5:48). This perfection is the maturity and completeness that characterizes the very nature of God Himself. New Testament writers repeatedly picked up the Old Testament theme, "Be holy, because I am holy" (1 Pet. 1:16, NIV), and applied it to moral concerns (see Rom. 12:1; Eph. 5:3; Col. 3:12; 1 Thess. 4:3-7; 2 Tim. 1:9; Heb. 12:14-16; 2 Pet. 3:11). The reality of this struggle in the church is evidenced by the fact that the Greek word for "sexual immorality" *(porneia)* and associated terms occur 55 times in 15 of the 27 books in the New Testament.

The hardness of human hearts caused by sin did not lead Jesus to give up on God's ideals (see Matt. 19:3-9). Jesus continually called His disciples to yield themselves to His lordship, not just in word, but also in deed. Living as citizens of God's kingdom, the disciples were taught to pray that God's will might "be done on earth as it is in heaven" (Matt. 6:10, NIV). That reign of God begins in each of our hearts and lives.

An Empowering Spirit

Believers do not wage their moral struggle alone. God has given us His Spirit as the Paraclete—the one who stands beside us (see John 14:15-17,26). The Holy Spirit is with us and in us forever, instructing us and reminding us of everything Jesus taught. The Spirit guides us into all truth (see John 16:13), helps us in our weakness (see Rom. 8:26), and enables us to put to death the misdeeds of the body (see Rom. 8:13). The Spirit enables us to translate our love for Christ into obedience.

Good News of Grace

The opening verses of Matthew's Gospel set the stage for the good news of what God can do in human hearts. Embedded within the tracing of Jesus' male ancestry are the names of four women who stand as testimony that God is able to triumph over human failure. Three of these women were involved in sexual sins. Tamar (see Matt. 1:3; compare Gen. 38) had disguised herself as a prostitute and engaged in sexual intercourse with her father-in-law in order to have children. Rahab (see Matt. 1:5; compare Josh. 2; 6), a Canaanite prostitute in the city of Jericho, was spared at the destruction of the city because she had protected the Israelite spies. Bathsheba (see Matt. 1:6; compare 2 Sam. 11), the wife of Uriah the Hittite, had engaged in an adulterous affair with King David. David had Uriah killed in order to cover his sin with her. Even the fourth woman, Ruth (see Matt. 1:5; compare Ruth 3), as a Moabite widow spent the night with Boaz in order to beseech him to fulfill his role as kinsman. In so doing, she did not commit sexual immorality, but did risk her reputation, which Boaz was careful to protect. These four served as a precursor to Matthew's account of the circumstances of a woman who became pregnant before her marriage.

The pregnant woman, of course, was Mary, the mother of Jesus. Though the Bible affirms that she conceived by the Holy Spirit and remained a virgin until after she gave birth to Jesus, accusations surely must have been made against her. For our purposes here, however, the point is that Matthew stressed God's ability to work through these situations to achieve His redemptive purposes. Even God's Holy One, the promised Messiah, though born of a virgin, had some ancestors who were tainted by sexual sin.

When we study the New Testament we find this pattern repeated time and time again: God deals redemptively with those involved in sexual sin.

• Recall the sinful woman to whom Jesus announced, "Your sins are forgiven" and "Your faith has saved you; go in peace" (Luke 7:48,50, NIV).

• Recall the Samaritan woman Jesus encountered at Jacob's well (John 4:4-42). Having been married to five husbands and living with a man to whom she was not married, she discovered the living water that only Jesus can offer. She believed and bore witness to Jesus' saving power.

• Recall the woman caught in the act of adultery brought before Jesus by accusers demanding her death (John 8:2-11). Jesus turned aside her accusers and refused to condemn her. "Go now and leave your life of sin," Jesus declared (John 8:11, NIV).

• Recall the man whom Paul encouraged the Corinthian church to discipline because he was sexually involved with his father's wife (1 Cor. 5:1-5). Though the discipline Paul recommended was severe, his ultimate goal was "that the sinful nature may be destroyed and his spirit saved on the day of the Lord" (1 Cor. 5:5, NIV).

The New Testament bears abundant testimony to the truth of God's promise that "If we confess our sins, he [God] is faithful and just and will forgive us our sins and purify us from all unrighteousness" (1 John 1:9, NIV). Sexual sins certainly are covered under that promise. We must not conclude from this, however, that sexual sins (or any other sins for that matter) are insignificant and can be engaged in casually. Indeed, the writer of Hebrews concluded that persons who "keep on sinning" after receiving the "knowledge of the truth" have no sacrifice left for their sins and are in reality "enemies of God" (Heb. 10:26-27, NIV).

Yet the New Testament tells a story of redemption and hope. The church is made up of persons who once were "sexually immoral," "adulterers," "male prostitutes," and "homosexual offenders." But through faith in Christ they have been "washed," "sanctified," and "justified in the name of the Lord Jesus Christ and by the Spirit of our God" (1 Cor. 6:11, NIV). Though our personal sins may not be named in that list, "sinner" applies to all of us. And all of us who believe have been washed, sanctified, and justified through Christ.

Thus, we can conclude with the words of Paul: "Flee from sexual immorality. All other sins a man commits are outside his body, but he who sins sexually sins against his own body. Do you not know that your body is a temple of the Holy Spirit, who is in you, whom you have received from God? You are not your own; you were bought at a price. Therefore honor God with your body" (1 Cor. 6:18-20, NIV).

These principles we must embrace. These convictions we must teach to our children. This truth we must live.

Understanding Your Child's Development

Wilson Wayne Grant

One of the most fascinating things about children is that they are never the same. They are ever changing, moving, expanding, learning, opening new facets of the personality—always responding to a built-in need of, and capacity for, growth. In fact, growth is *the* key element of children from birth to adulthood.

Luke 2:52 gives us a glimpse of the childhood of Jesus. Luke tells us that "Jesus grew in wisdom and stature, and in favor with God and men (NIV)." Although this Scripture refers specifically to Jesus, it describes the principal tasks of all children: to grow in mind, body, and spirit. An interdependence exists between body, mind, and spirit. Growth in one area affects growth in all the others. Luke implies that the total personality is important in God's plan. God made our body along with the rest of our being, and He expects parents to nurture body and mind along with spirit.

Built-in Drive to Grow

Children have a built-in drive to learn and grow. Physical growth plunges forward imploringly but so does mental and emotional growth. The baby begins to explore his world immediately after birth as his eyes dart about the newly expanded environment. The baby begins his exploration of his intimate world with his most useful tool, the mouth. Soon he is reaching, touching, grasping. Then he is rolling, scooting, crawling, and walking. As his language develops, new avenues of exploration open up as he interacts with his world using this most complex of all tools. The toddler's persistent questioning is an example of the child's push to keep expanding his knowledge about everything. The drive to learn and grow is seen in the school-age child's thirst for knowledge and the teenager's search for independence and mastery of his world.

This innate drive to learn and grow persists in all children unless turned off by negative, hurtful responses from the world around them. The drive can be turned off by making the learning process painful, unrewarding, boring, or anxiety-provoking. For instance, the infant whose natural coos meet silence and unresponsiveness will gradually make fewer and fewer sounds. If the preschool child's enthusiastic and incessant questions are met with indifference or hostility, the child will likely ask fewer and fewer questions to the point that the innate desire to learn is severely dulled. The school-age child who keeps on failing eventually quits trying.

Growth is most impressive during the early years. The average newborn weighs seven and a half pounds and is 20 inches long. By six months, the child has doubled its weight and will triple it in one year. Growth in height is just as spectacular. By age two, the average child will reach one-half of his adult height. The body proportions also change drastically as the child passes from infancy to puberty to adulthood. At birth the head is proportionally much larger than in the adult comprising one-third of the body's length. Arms, legs, trunk, genitalia all change in size and shape through the growth cycle.

Growth Varies

The pace of growth is characterized by rapid spurts and level plateaus. One year, our son hardly grew at all for nine months. Then he shot up two inches in six months, outgrowing all of his clothes. All children do not grow at the same rate. Each stage of childhood has an average, an upper, and a lower range of normal. Normal is a range, not a point on a line. An average eight-year old weighs 55 pounds, but one weighing forty-six or sixty-five pounds is also normal.

Parents are often worried about variations in growth, feeling compelled to compare their child's growth with that of other children. If cousin Janie walks a month before Jim, his parents are likely to be concerned. When Susan's friend of the same age begins to have a menstrual period before Susan even has breast development, Susan, as well as her parents, wonder. But such variations are normal.

Forcing or pushing our children into some expected "average" is not needed. We cannot stretch our children to make them taller, nor force them to do certain things. Growth in mind, spirit, and stature cannot be pushed. What parents can do is provide an atmosphere that allows and encourages growth in all areas and then give children room to develop at their own pace.

Concept of Basic Needs

Each stage of life presents the individual with basic needs and tasks. Working through the task of each developmental stage before the next stage of development can be successfully tackled is necessary. Only as the basic developmental needs are met can the child move toward maturity. (See the developmental chart at the end of this chapter.)

The Infant

The infant, totally dependent at birth, is a perfect example of the insurmountable drive toward growth. Growth during the first year is phenomenal. Babies rapidly gain control over their bodies. At first they search their environment by moving their heads and eyes. But in only a few short weeks they are reaching out and grasping with their hands. Then in only a short time they are sitting up, then scooting and crawling only soon to stand up and cruise and walk. By three or four weeks infants smile when satisfied. By two or three months, they smile when their parents smile at them. Babies coo, babble, and soon make sounds that everyone interprets as real words.

Many people believe that babies have no cares or worries at all, but evidence shows that they are subject to many of the moods, worries, fears, and disappointments adults experience. Babies do not worry in the same way as a business executive or a farmer worries—a baby's feelings are more tentative, less mature, but they are feelings none-the-less. Babies are happy when they get attention; they can become depressed when left by their familiar caretaker; they sense nervousness in others and become nervous and restless themselves. Recognizing the existence of such feelings will enable parents and other important adults to meet the child's needs more appropriately.

Primary among the baby's basic needs is the need to experience love and trust. This is expressed in stable caretakers who hold, cuddle, feed, and talk to them. Physical touch, eye contact, and soothing verbal stimulation are key elements in giving a child a sense of warmth and security. An example of this is the act of nursing and feeding the infant. Feeding is important to the child for two reasons. Not only does it provide nutrition, but the physical closeness, whether from breast or bottle, gives the infant a feeling of pleasure, trust, and security. Persons who do not experience love and affirmation early in life often have trouble forming deep, loving relationships as adults. Such love and affirmation is important in helping the child develop his full potential, personally and intellectually.

Infants experience their sexuality early on as they are imprinted with a sense of being a boy or a girl. They experience sexual stimulation as they accidentally touch their genitals as seen in the erection of a baby boy's penis. A child's attitude about his or her body germinates early in life as the child senses approval or disapproval of his or her body by important people in his life. Learning to experience love and trust is the first step in developing a healthy sexuality. Only as the babies receive love and trust will they be able to grow into adults who can successfully express love to others.

From Toddler to Preschooler

Toddlers run, literally, from infancy. Mobile and curious, they are everywhere, bundles of energy, exploring every nook of their environment.

Having experienced affirmation through love and trust as an infant, toddlers' main thrust is to attain psychological independence and personal identity. Having acquired some measure of language, their favorite word is *"no."* It is an expression of independent thinking. The next favorite word is *"me."* "Give it me!" or "Me do it myself!" are favorite phrases.

The tumbling, active, impulsive toddler evolves imperceptibly into the preschooler who is more social and verbal and in control. Among the important developmental tasks of the preschooler is the learning of control over bodily functions in a way that is acceptable to the society in which he lives. An important part of this control involves toilet training which is a necessary step on the journey to mastery as well as social acceptance.

Some parents approach toilet training with anxiety and even fear because they have heard how their child can be ruined if they make a mistake. Others just don't know how to get started. Some fear that their child is abnormal because he or she is not trained as quickly as the little boy or girl next door.

In general, toddlers are not ready for toilet training until two years or later because it is around this age that they acquire sufficient language skills to understand and motor skills that allow them to control their body. By using a gentle and encouraging approach, and terms that clearly communicate what you want, training is usually accomplished with a minimal amount of fuss. This is an excellent time to begin to teach them the right terms for different body parts and functions.

The Older Preschooler

Somewhere around four or five years, the young child begins to bombard significant adults with questions. Every sentence seems to begin with why, how, or what. Sooner or later this curiosity will touch on concerns about where they came from and how they got here. One normal question at age four is, "Where did I come from?" With this question the child may be asking any one of a number of things. One way of getting at what the child really wants to know is to ask, "What do you mean?" The child's response to this question will let you know if he is inquiring about birth or whether he is asking a theological question ("Who made me?") or a geographic question ("Did I come from Alabama like Johnny?")

In fact, this question, "What do you mean?" is one of the best tools parents have in teaching their child of any age about sex. By asking this, the parent learns where the child is coming from and has some idea of his or her level of understanding. The parent can then build on what the child reveals about what is already known.

The preschooler's curiosity extends to the body and how it works. They ask questions about it: "What is my belly button for?" "Why am I different from Julie?" They are discovering their bodies. At this age, this is quite common and natural. Parents should not be frightened or concerned if their boy or girl touches or plays with their genitalia while taking a bath or getting ready for bed. A child who does this in public should be corrected gently but not scolded. You might say something like, "It is better not to touch yourself like that." The parent is giving the child some guidelines for behavior but not making him or her feel guilty or bad.

As infants stumble into toddlerhood, their motor control is uncertain and unsteady at first but improves steadily through the preschool years. By and large, through play the preschooler hones these skills. Running, jumping, and tricycle-riding are all means of improving and developing gross motor, or balance, skills. Drawing, coloring, cutting, and working puzzles are ways they develop fine motor skills.

Self-control is an ongoing quest at this age. Learning to control ourselves is perhaps one of the most important and most difficult tasks humans face. The entire human adventure is one long story of the victories gained when we control ourselves and the defeats we suffer when we do not. The impulsive, self-centered toddler should merge into a preschooler with some beginning ability to delay gratification, to stop and think before acting, and to have some consideration of others.

When we speak of teaching a child self-control, we mean helping the preschooler to achieve a quality of mind that cannot and should not be absolutely rigid. What we strive for is the right kind of self-control, not one that cripples. Proper self-control is the process of learning to accept, among other things, delay and frustration. The infant tolerates no delay between desire and realization. For example, if he is hungry, he wants food now. If he is left alone, of course, he will starve. The healthy adult, on the other hand, has learned not only to accept delays, but also to anticipate his needs and plan for their satisfaction. A parent can help the child move toward this kind of control by not giving in to inappropriate demands.

By the early preschool years, the child's sexual identity is well-formed. We never think of a baby as just a baby—we think of it as a he or a she. A baby is not an "it." The Bible states in Genesis 1:27 that "God created man in his own image, in the image of God he created him; male and female he created them." Men and women have always been acutely aware of their masculinity and femininity, and this awareness dawns at an early age. Each sex has characteristics that distinguish one from the other. The most obvious difference is sexual organs and sexual functions. Secondary sexual characteristics such as breasts, hair distribution, body shape, and pitch of voice identify one sex from the other in a physical way. Each sex has subtle, unique psychological characteristics.

Although hereditary factors and hormones play a role in how a person feels about his sexual identity, experience and nurture also play a role. Gender identity is defined as all those things that a person says or does to disclose himself or herself as being either a boy or a girl. A person's concept of his or her sexual identity, apart from the physical characteristics of being male and female, is derived from how he or she was treated and the role models observed growing up. In a real sense one learns to be a boy or girl and, thus, a man or woman from role models early in life.

The preschool child's moral reasoning is on what is called the preconventional level. The child's thinking is concrete and limited to what he feels, sees, and hears. "I won't misbehave because I will get into trouble." While wanting to stay out of trouble, he might think of violating a rule if he thinks he won't get caught. At this age his thinking is still primarily self-centered thinking of his own wants, needs, and wishes before others.

The School-age Child

The elementary school age period of a child's life extends from six years of age to puberty. In many ways this is a relatively quiet period of development compared to the tornado of the preschool period and what is to come in adolescence. The rate of physical growth lessens, and a stable personality percolates to the surface. The intensity of family ties is diluted by the world of friends, teachers, and other adults. Parents are no longer the only important adults in the child's life. Much of the curiosity formerly invested in his own body and the immediate world around him broadens to take in a larger world—sports, clubs, friends, learning baseball averages, and exploring fantasy stories.

Muscular coordination matures, enabling the child to learn to ride a bike, bake a cake, dive, and pitch a no-hitter. Emotional control stabilizes, and the boy or girl is able to postpone gratification—at least part of the time—if given a good reason. The child is able to make stable friendships and enjoys group activities, particularly with the same sex.

This is a period of rapid intellectual growth. The child's great thirst for knowledge is satisfied through school, reading, hobbies, and group activities. The child's boundless energy can be rather easily channeled into worthwhile pursuits. The child is interested in the facts of any situation and often questions statements to make sure they are true. The school-age child wants, and is able to make, limited choices. Parents can profit by giving the school-age child many opportunities to make decisions. This will build self-esteem as well as provide experience for making much more difficult and important decisions later. The child is not yet equipped to go without supervision but can make decisions about many day-to-day activities.

As a preschooler, the child primarily lived within the cocoon of the family. Now, however, the child is thrust into the world where much of the day is spent away from the security of the family. The child needs to learn how to relate and cooperate with peers of both sexes and learn the appropriate sex role. In other words, the child learns what behavior is and is not appropriate. The school-age child will continue to need varying amounts of supervision. Turning the preteen child loose too soon without guidelines or control is dangerous. But another danger is to smother the school-age child with over-protection without allowing the child to make decisions.

The school-age child's primary developmental task is to learn about the world and how to relate to other people. These tasks are accomplished through formal education as well as through play and organized activities.

Later, in the preadolescent period, moral reasoning is approaching the conventional level. At this level, the child is concerned with maintaining social order because "it is the right thing to do." The preteen rather inflexibly accepts the perceived group standard and is beginning to accept some personal responsibility for actions. At this stage the child is quite vulnerable to peer pressure, both positive and negative. Thus environmental influences are important in determining values. The preteen is open to, and influenced by, the basic rules of morality. Actions are either right or wrong.

The intense sexual curiosity of the preschool years is to a great degree turned to other pursuits by the school-age child. The child is more interested in exploring the environment and absorbing facts than being concerned with sexual matters. Sexual questions are fewer and more matter-of-fact. Modesty becomes important. The child naturally wants to keep covered and is not nearly as interested in bare bodies and genitals as before or will be later. Sexual interests are not dormant, however, they simply are more diffused and covered by other interests. While they are partly channeled into new interests and skills, they are also better concealed from adult eyes. Reading permits independent investigation into dictionaries and other sources for sexual information. Age mates may at some point become research partners in the game of, "I'll show you mine if you'll show me yours."

Children of this age do have questions about sexual matters although they do not always verbalize them. Common concerns are the origin of babies, the process of birth, the father's role in reproduction, the sex organs and their functions, and marriage. Great detail is unnecessary and often confusing. Answer each question simply but adequately allowing the child to ask other questions as desired.

By *ten* or *eleven* years, many children who have not received adequate instructions about the facts of sexuality become disturbed and worry about what is real. They usually have heard bits and pieces of facts from peers. Preadolescents need to know about the bodily changes they are about to experience for the onset of puberty is unpredictable and can come at varying ages. Preadolescent boys and girls need to be instructed about menstruation, development of breasts, changes in body shape, and changes in genital organs. The girl of *nine* or *ten* will hear whispered references to menstruation and will probably have friends who start their periods as early as nine years.

The school-age child's relative calm emotional development and increasing intellectual comprehension makes this a time to learn the major facts of reproduction. Some parents delay giving the child information about sex as if not talking about it will delay the onset of puberty and adolescence. The fact is, however, that the upheaval of adolescence will be much more tumultuous and difficult in the face of ignorance. The glandular clock cannot be stopped or turned back. Some parents, never having experienced proper preparation themselves, feel helpless, not able to find the right words, right time, and right way to talk with the preteen. One of the purposes of this book is to give parents tools and the confidence to make this job easier.

Adolescence

Adolescence is a confusing time of life. Roughly paralleling the teenage years, it spans that part of a person's life between childhood and adulthood during which he is neither an adult nor a child. The outstanding characteristic of adolescence is change with accelerated physical, intellectual, sexual, and emotional growth. The dawn of adolescence throws major challenges at the growing child as well as at his or her parents. Parents often anticipate this step in their child's growth with some anxiety and fear. Neither child nor parent can know exactly what to expect.

An increase in length of body with stretching of arms and legs is usually the first sign that puberty is occurring. This rapid acceleration in growth is due to the outpouring of hormones into the bloodstream. This process begins earlier in girls than in boys. Thus during the early stages of adolescence, girls tend to be taller than boys of the same age. However, the female hormone estrogen slows the growth in girls around age *fourteen* or *fifteen* years while boys continue to grow. Near the mid-teen years, boys begin to grow taller than their female peers.

Soon after growth accelerates, the sex organs in both girls and boys begin to mature. At birth the internal and external sex organs of both sexes are well-defined but immature. At puberty the genitals begin to mature, to increase in size as well as in their ability to function.

Hormones released by the growing genitals signal the development of secondary sexual characteristics. For example, the female body contour takes on a more mature woman appearance, and the breasts enlarge. In boys, the voice deepens as facial and body hair thicken and muscles bulge. Both boys and girls develop the characteristic male or female pattern of body hair. Eventually boys are able to produce sperm, and girls begin to ovulate and menstruate. Through this growth process, their bodies are now ready for reproduction. This point in time is called puberty.

The age of puberty is variable and dependent on racial, climatal, emotional, nutritional, and cultural factors. Puberty occurs earlier in warmer than in colder climates. Inadequate nutrition and poor health may delay it.

By late adolescence, rapid physical growth ceases, and the body becomes more familiar and predictable. Adolescents are now more comfortable with themselves, and it becomes easier for them to control their emotions. Having explored a variety of roles, values, and interests, a personal commitment to some of these will have been made.

Even when well-prepared, most adolescents experience mixed feelings as a once familiar body changes almost daily. Budding breasts to the girl and bulging biceps to the boy may be welcomed. But pimples are not. Breast development may seem too much too soon or too little too late. The adolescent is constantly wondering what others think of his or her appearance. He is somewhat yet uncertain about any bodily change that hints at his developing sexuality. During this time of early adolescence, physical education, undressing, and communal showers can trigger an emotional crisis.

Along with these monumental changes in anatomy and the physiology of adolescents is an awakening sexual excitability. An intense interest in the opposite sex develops. To some extent all of life and relationships are colored by this sexual interest. The same hormones that produce bodily changes are also stirring up sexual feelings and thoughts that cannot be hidden. A glance or touch can create sexual excitement. Double meanings are read into the most casual remarks. This physical and emotional change of puberty demands that each individual come to terms with a changing body as well as sexual conflicts and desires.

Christian adolescents experience the same sexual impulses as other young people. They know that if some of their impulses were carried out, harm to themselves and others would be the result. They cannot deny their feelings, yet they honestly want to do what is right. They are caught asking themselves, "Who is the real me?"

Parents should not be shocked by their adolescent's sexual changes and interests. These are inevitable and normal. As a matter of fact, the adolescents who do not seem interested in sexual matters are the ones who may have problems because they are probably hiding their real feelings and not learning healthy ways to express their emotions.

If parents stay calm, present the adolescent with healthy models of sexuality, and stand ready to talk about the issues, the adolescent will likely surprise them by the ability to work through the ups and downs and actually "grow up." Indeed most adolescents are struggling to deal with the conflicts they are experiencing. They need firm and well-defined limits, but they also need support, love, and encouragement. They will make mistakes, wrong judgments and will overreact because they are still growing. But the underlying drive is to maturity and responsibility.

The healthy adolescent can reason abstractly, taking into account consequences of behavior that are not concrete or presently visible. Simple rules of right and wrong no longer satisfy him or her. To know the "why" behind the rules is needed. The focus moves from the act of behavior to relationships, motives, and consequences. The capacity to live by abstract moral and ethical principles and think of others as well as oneself is present. A full commitment to religious principles can be made at this level.

The primary task of adolescence is to attain emotional independence from parents and come to grips with their personal identity. This is a process that occurs over time with many ups and downs. But by the late teen years, healthy individuals will have developed a stable self-image that will allow them to move to adulthood as persons who can think for themselves and make a positive contribution to society. At this point, parents will have done their job although their concern and interest in their "product" never ceases.

DEVELOPMENTAL CHART OF SEXUAL CHARACTERISTICS IN BOYS AND GIRLS
Norma Stevens

Characteristic	Boy's Age Span	Girl's Age Span
Beginning breast development		8-13
Appearance of pubic hair	10-15	11-12
Appearance of armpit hair	12-17	12-13
Onset of menstruation		9-18
Beginning growth of scrotum and testes	11-13	
Beginning growth of penis	10-15	
First ejaculation	11-15	
Voice begins to deepen	13-16	11-18

PARENT AND CHILD DEVELOPMENT CHART
Wilson Wayne Grant

AGE	DEVELOPMENTAL TASKS	CHARACTERISTICS	PARENTAL TASKS
Infant (0-18 months)	Experience love and trust Accomplish motor skills Begin language development	Totally dependent Rapid physical growth Emotionally one with parent	Learn the cues and interpret needs
Toddler (1.5 to 3 yrs)	Attain sense of independence Attain control of body functions	Mobile, curious, active Asserts independence Acquires speech skills	Accept the loss of full control while asserting limits Develop sense of separate identity
Preschool (4-5 yrs)	Attain initiative Attain self-control Perfect basic motor and speech skills	Incessant questions Wants to know about emotional, sexual, and spiritual things	Learn to separate Accept growth

Stage	Developmental tasks	Characteristics	Parental role
School-age (6–11 yrs)	Learn basic facts Learn to relate to people outside of family Develop sense of fair play	Industrious Wants to make choices	Accept rejection Be there when needed and not intrude Discuss consequences of decisions and choices
Adolescent (12 yrs to adulthood)	Acquire sense of identity Acquire independence from family Learn to live with sexuality	Peer oriented Emotional Self-conscious Changeable Establishes own set of values	Appropriately let go Learn to build new life as children leave Learn to relate to children as adults

Knowing Who You Are as a Parent

Susan Lanford

Who are you as a parent? You may be twenty-one years old with a new-born baby or fifty years old with two teenagers and a school-age child. Whatever your age may be or that of your children, it is important for you to get in touch with the attitudes and opinions you hold if you expect to communicate effectively with your children about sexual matters.

Knowing My Inner Thoughts

Let's stop and study some attitudes that persist among Christian parents. Do you find yourself in any of them? Parent, now is the time to truly seek to know yourself.

"I'm Afraid."

This is probably the universal on the list—fear. If we're going to conquer fear, we've got to face the source(s) of our fear in specifics.

Are you afraid that if you talk about sex your kids will become sexually active? The current is already flowing in that direction. The statistics for Christian adolescents are truly something to ponder and fear. For example, one study of teenagers in evangelical churches reported:

- By eighteen years of age, 43% have had sexual intercourse; 65% have had some kind of sexual contact, from fondling breasts to sexual intercourse
- 39% see fondling breasts as sometimes morally acceptable
- 32% see fondling genitals as sometimes morally acceptable
- 35% could **not** state that premarital sexual intercourse is **always** morally unacceptable[1]

Are you afraid you'll be too embarrassed to do a good job of it? Talk about more than body parts and reproduction. Include your feelings about being a man or a woman. Tell anecdotes about how you were taught the truth about sexuality. Many adults are still sorting out the truth. And if you're embarrassed, say so. And keep talking.

Are you afraid your kids will be too embarrassed to really listen to you? Remember, this is no time for monologues. Encourage their questions, read and discuss Bible verses together, bring pictures to examine. And don't try to tell them everything you know in one sitting. Your children may seem embarrassed, but make no mistake, they will be listening.

"I'm Confused."

The television documentary's tag line, "Read More About It," is appropriately repeated here. Bone up on your terminology and pronunciations. Read carefully and thoroughly the corresponding book your child or youth is reading and any other helps you plan to use before initiating conversations with your children. If it helps, think of this extra reading as a refresher course in a subject you know but studied a long time ago.

Part of easing your sense of confusion is to study again what the Bible teaches about sexuality. You will want to study that section in this book again and become familiar with it.

"I Don't Need To."

Sometimes our children will give us the impression that they have absolutely no interest in sexual information. Don't be fooled by those innocent faces and Cheshire cat smiles! There are oodles of questions in their minds, but not very many questions being asked with their mouths.

A bit more seriously, take another look on the outside. The physical changes that occur are the first stages of the sexual maturing of their bodies. They will reach sexual maturity from a purely physiological standpoint long before they are emotionally or spiritually mature enough for responsible sexual behavior. Without clear guidance, they will act more from instinct, more in line with the typically bad information from their other sources of sexual information (and they do have them).

One other thought about taking the initiative in instructing your children about their sexuality. Christian parents are the primary conduit of God's truth to their children. The Bible makes it clear that parents are best suited to instruct and disciple their children. Being Christ's disciple means that we grow more like Him, and that we honor Him in every aspect of our lives. Teaching our children about God's design for them as sexual beings is part of our God-given parenting task as disciplers of our children.

"I'm Guilty."

You may be feeling guilt on two different levels. First, guilty because you've done little or nothing regarding sex education with your children. Let's deal with that a moment.

Remember, and take heart:

• Your nurturing, loving attitudes and behaviors have conveyed nonverbally to your children their worth.

• Expressions of love between you and your spouse in their presence model God's gift of marriage in a positive, warm way.

• Anytime you've dealt honestly, even in your embarrassment, to the "Where do babies come from?" and related questions, you've been educating your children.

Words will only build on what your behaviors and attitudes have taught them. But be assured, they need to *hear* you, because their sources of misinformation are plenty.

Still feel like you haven't done enough? A famous comedian, reflecting on his life, once said, "Eighty percent of success is just showing up!" I like that! It reminds me to start!

Second, your source of guilt may harken back to your personal involvement in some sexual sin. You may feel you've disqualified yourself forever as your children's instructor about sexuality. Let's deal with this, too. One family counselor noted:

> "Sexual sin has a way of haunting us. When we least expect it, the memories assault our minds and emotions, causing us to classify ourselves as worthless failures. Furthermore, the past can distort our present perspective on sex, leading us to seriously question our ability to teach our children the unadulterated truth. The question lingers: Can someone who failed teach someone else to succeed?"[2]

There is at least one biblical anecdote to assure us that we can teach in an area where we've experienced failure.

The sin of David with Bathsheba is probably his most famous sin. In his great psalm of confession, David pleads for purity again and promises God: "Then I will teach transgressors your ways, and sinners will turn back to you" (Ps. 51:13, NIV). David must have sensed that his terrible sin against Bathsheba and against God was forgiven. And from the pure vantage point of forgiveness, David wanted to teach others that God's way was the best of all. Isn't it interesting that the Lord preserved for us the words of one of David's "students," his own son Solomon?

"When I was a boy in my father's house, still tender, and an only child of my mother, he taught me and said, 'Lay hold of my words with all your heart; keep my commands and you will live. Get wisdom, get understanding; do not forget my words or swerve from them'"(Prov. 4:3-5, NIV).

Solomon, the son of David, found the teaching of his father so powerful and convicting that he recorded it and testified to it as an adult.

John Nieder suggests that our children can either benefit from our past sin or be plagued by it. The choice is ours to make. He offers these steps in finding again God's forgiveness and experiencing His restoration of joy in your life:

1. Ask God to forgive you and believe that He has. Live like the promise of 1 John 1:9, that if you confess your sins, you are forgiven by God, and God has taken hold of and changed your life.

2. Commit yourself to a life of personal purity. As He advised the adulterous woman, Jesus says to you today, "Go, and sin no more." Knowing what the Bible teaches about sexuality equips you to take the path of personal purity.

3. Forgive yourself. Think of yourself the same way God does. After all, this brought you to the recognition of your own need to repent of your sin. God sees us and loves us. God hears our initial prayer of repentance for salvation and calls us His children. God looks at our sin and sees a barrier between us and Him. God answers our cry of confession and sees us "whiter than snow," our sins as far from us as "the east is from the west." You will never be more in tune with Him than in seeing yourself and your world from His perspective.

4. Forget the past and press on for the prize (Phil. 3:13). The only things worth remembering from a sinful experience are the lessons you learn about yourself, about the world you live in, and about God's presence in your life. The most important task to which to dedicate your spiritual energies is daily "running the race," His race, in a way that will bring God honor.

5. Look for the good that God can bring from your past. Did you marry because of an unplanned pregnancy? You can tell your child firsthand about sexual passion out of control or the consequence of doing what your friends were doing sexually. Did you use pornographic materials for your sex education? You can describe the vast difference between the world's abuse of people for temporary stimulation and God's good gift of sexuality as He planned it for a lifetime.[3]

Your sexual sin may not be appropriate to discuss in detail with your children at any age. But letting them know that you tried life from the world's point of view and found it inadequate, or frustrating, or poisonous, or evil in your life is a powerful testimony that only you can give them. Remember: the guilt with which you struggle over past sins is *God's good gift to you.* It is His way of helping you see that problem the way He does—as sin. It is His way of bringing you to confession, for He longs to forgive you and restore the joy of your salvation.

Knowing the Sexual Me

We adults rarely reach a place of perfect knowledge in any area of our lives. This is true regarding our own growth and development. Reaching adulthood is *not* like stepping onto a wide, flat plateau that stretches for miles and miles and never changes. We will continue to change throughout life. One area in which we change is understanding our own sexuality.

We married folk would do well to tend to our sexual needs. A husband and wife, in a loving relationship, are the best instructors in how to grow sexually in marriage. There is a book in this series just for us: *Celebrating Sex in Your Marriage* by Dan and Sandra McGee. Read it and grow in your relationship. Meanwhile, here are a few reminders that will help us all.

- **Make your bed a haven from the hassles of everyday life.**

We're all busy people. No parent has extra time! More than likely, you're finding money, patience, and leisure are also in short supply! That means that lovemaking most often occurs at the end of the day when a couple finally falls or crawls into bed. Don't continue an argument there, or solve the latest parenting dilemma, or plan the summer vacation. Let this time and place be protected as a safe place where you comfort each other, hold each other, and regain intimacy with each other.

• **Growing an intimate marriage is more important, and _more satisfying_, than the physical act of intercourse**. The mystery and beauty of the biblical injunction "and the two shall become one flesh" is so much more than physical intimacy. In fact, one writer of long ago described intimacy by saying:

> Oh, the comfort, the inexpressible comfort of feeling safe with a person; having neither to weigh thoughts nor measure words, but to pour them all out, just as they are, chaff and grain together, knowing that a faithful hand will take and sift them, keep what is worth keeping, and then, with a breath of kindness, blow the rest away.[4]

This is deep, lasting respect and friendship. It will endure and mean more than intercourse alone ever will.

• **Remember: Marriage gives you more power than any other relationship in your life.** My husband and I often say to participants in a marriage enrichment setting: "The good news in marriage is—your spouse knows you better than anyone else in the whole world! The bad news in marriage is—your spouse knows you better than anyone else in the whole world!" You derive this incredible power from the growing intimacy just described. You also derive this power as a gift from your spouse. Anytime we commandeer that power and use it in hurtful, manipulative ways, intimacy is destroyed. The sexual side of marriage is one arena where our incredible power over our spouse is easily abused. Remember the teaching to the Corinthian Christians: "The wife's body does not belong to her alone but also to her husband. In the same way, the husband's body does not belong to him alone but also to his wife" (1 Cor. 7:4, NIV).

• **Marriage is as much a spiritual union as a physical union.** How often have you heard the Scriptures quoted during a wedding ceremony, "Therefore what God has joined together, let man not separate" (Matt. 19:6, NIV). Paul's classic passage on roles of husbands and wives is Ephesians 5:21-33. Paul gives us a clue of his meaning in the passage when he says, "I am talking about Christ and the church" (Eph. 5:32, NIV). He used the earthly relationship of marriage to try and explain the spiritual relationship of Christ and the church, and he sums it all up by saying, "This is a _profound mystery!_" (Eph. 5:32, NIV, my emphasis added). Because marriage is spiritual, there will always be a sense of mystery to it—the complexity of the relationship, the dimensions of purpose, the expressions of commitment. We never figure it all out in our married life. But the mystery itself is God's good gift to us. We will never understand all that marriage and our spouse mean to us. What a fulfilling, interesting way to spend a lifetime—delving daily into the mystery!

Since marriage is both spiritual and physical, see how practically Scripture instructs the married folk: "Do not deprive each other except by mutual consent and for a time, so that you may devote yourselves to prayer. Then come together again so that Satan will not tempt you because of your lack of self-control" (1 Cor. 7:5, NIV).

• **Most importantly, adopt God's view of sexuality in your marriage and His view of your spouse**. If you have never done a systematic study of the Scriptures to learn God's view of sexuality, plan a time now, ideally with your spouse, and learn again how God views you two and your marriage. Covenant together to examine your married life from His vantage point.

In particular, read together the Song of Songs. Probably it has not been the subject of many sermons or Bible studies in your recent experience. It is beautifully, explicitly, poetically celebrating the gift of human sexuality in the exclusive relationship of marriage. It describes the doubts we all have about our attractiveness to our spouse and the joys of feeling attracted to our spouse. It details the pain of separation and the delight of reunion with the beloved. It clearly revels in a love so completely expressed that nothing sexually is available to persons outside the marriage. Yes—it's all in your Bible! And it can be a very enriching experience to read it to and with your spouse. Remind yourselves afresh, with these ancient words, of the beauty and mystery of physical, sexual love between a groom and bride.

What about sex and the single parent? Potentially, the marriage relationship is one where a man or woman can receive the greatest confirmation that they are loved, cared for, valued and valuable to another person. When that relationship is gone, much of the personal affirmation we all need may go, too. The trap for the single parent is sometimes concluding that sexual encounters will meet personal needs for affirmation. We need the intimacy and affirmation and hope that physical sexual expressions provide them.

I have not walked your path. I don't know the absolute verity of what I've read. Let me simply report that the consensus of Christians writing about sex for single parents is this. Continue to uphold God's plan for physical expressions of sexuality only in the marriage relationship. You'll never match your walk and your talk in teaching your child about sexuality if you do not.

Being single again does not change your sexual nature. Lenore Buth writes this encouragement to Christian single parents:

Psychologists say sexual expression is a primary human need, second only to food. Research also shows, however, that putting off one's sexual needs does not damage a person, either physically or emotionally. Nor does it eventually cause distorted personality traits. There are millions of single persons who are perfectly well-adjusted and fulfilled without having a sexual relationship. Christian counselors would agree with those conclusions, but add another dimension. They point out that Christ's grace and strength are sufficient for all our needs and that one's sexual desires can be put aside for a time with no damage.[5]

The challenge to single parents is the one we all need to accept and model: "I have the strength to face all conditions by the power that Christ gives me" (Phil. 4:13, GNB).

Recognizing the Parent Trap!

1. Accept the fact, or rather the raw truth, that your child is not parented by a perfect parent. Once you've accepted that, you'll find there is grace for those days when your parenting is good enough—no more and no less.

2. As a Christian parent, you have a rare, continuing insight into the world of your child, because you are your Father's child. We know it is natural and most healthy for children to grow into teenagers and into adults, capable of life independent from their parents. We want this progression for our children, some days more than others! But as God's child, we never become so mature that He sends us out of His family to live independently from Him. Till the day we die, we are forever our Father's child. And if we tend our spiritual life regularly, then we still know what it means to be corrected, disciplined, guided, taught, and encouraged by our heavenly parent. Use those insights to keep you sensitive to how it feels to be parented. You and your child may have more common experiences than either of you has realized.

3. Remember, the bottom line for all good parenting is what builds independence, esteem, and self-discipline in your child. It is *not* what builds regard, esteem, or praise for you as the parent. Your child and her life are at stake in the parenting process, not you and your life.

Notes

[1] John Nieder, *What to Tell Your Child About Sex.* (Nashville: Thomas Nelson Publishers, 1991) 19.

[2] Ibid. 33.

[3] Ibid. 33-35.

[4] George Eliot, quoted in Kathy Lipscomb Bridge, *Sex Education for the 90's.* (Portland, Maine: J. Weston Walch, Publishers, 1991) 73.

[5] Lenore Buth, *How to Talk Confidently With Your Child About Sex.* (St. Louis: Concordia Publishing House, 1988) 34.

Just for Parents of Young Children

Ellen Chambers

Boys and Girls—Alike and Different was written for you to use with your young child. When your child shows an interest in or has a question about himself or the creation of babies, you should use that teachable moment to share the book with him. As you do, be aware of his interest. If he is very young, his attention span may be short. Do not force him to finish the book or even a section in one reading. Stop when he chooses. Associating happy times with reading the book is important to his wanting to read again.

You can use just the pictures in the book. Your young child may have asked a question that a picture could help answer. You may choose to use several pictures at a particular reading.

Young children learn through repetition. Be prepared to enthusiastically reread the book. It gets old and dull to you, but to your young child it provides assurance, pleasure, and knowledge. With each reading, your child learns that the information will not change, thus reinforcing learning.

A Gift from God

In Psalm 127:3 we are reminded that children are a heritage from the Lord. Your child is truly a gift, a precious trust. Jesus reminds us just how precious children are. Mark 10:13-15 tells us of a time Jesus scolded the disciples for turning the children away. Jesus welcomed the children. He touched them, held them, and blessed them. The children were used to illustrate the kind of trusting faith we as adults must have.

How precious and how frightening to behold a new life. You are going to be primarily responsible for what your child becomes. Your child is like wet, soft clay. How will you shape and mold him or her?

Lessons in Sexuality

Your baby is a young child now. So for several years you have been providing sex education whether you knew it or not.

When your child was an infant in diapers, how did you react to a messy diaper? Did you moan and groan and make all manner of contortions with your face and nose? Was your reaction different when the diaper was just wet?

If you reacted negatively toward changing your child's diaper, you were sending a message that bodily functions were bad. Your child may also have interpreted your displeasure of changing diapers (especially dirty ones) as his being naughty to have produced such a mess.

But when you pleasantly undertook the task of keeping your baby clean and comfortable, you communicated a far different set of feelings. You said with your attitude that the bodily functions were normal and not to be considered wrong. Therefore, your child also accepted her bodily functions as normal.

Then the great adventure of toilet training happened. It is usually one of two extremes: a pleasant experience or a miserable experience. Parents' experiences with toilet training, whether positive or negative, are influenced by many factors. For example: Was your child ready to be trained? Were you pressured into training your child as a convenience (no more diapers)? Did you try to force your child to perform in the commode? Were you frustrated because of your lack of knowledge in toilet training? Again, your attitude about bodily functions is being interpreted by your child as his having goodness or a lack of goodness.

At four or five she still may have been or be wetting the bed at night occasionally. There still may be accidents during the day. What is your response when this happens? Consider why it happens.

Did you allow your child to have a large quantity to drink right before bedtime? If so, there was no time for the liquid to be expelled while he was awake. Is your child a sound sleeper? Wet sheets may not be enough to wake your child, not to mention the physical urge that signals the need to urinate.

Why so much about diapering, toilet training, and accidents? Because these activities are directly related to each of us and our attitude about our bodily functions. For the young child, the genital area is associated with elimination. Our attitude about our bodily functions affects what we think about ourselves. And what we think about ourselves stays with us for a lifetime!

The young child is naturally curious. He explores, questions, and tries to take apart his world. As he ventures out, he will begin to be curious about the opposite sex and concerned about the baby in Mrs. Watson's stomach (his idea of where a baby is located).

As a parent you may be uncomfortable with the exploration and questions about his body and babies. It is important that you be at ease with such topics for the sake of your child. Being curious about the penis or the vagina is normal and to be expected.

His curiosity naturally leads to exploration. Through exploration he discovers pleasant feelings when touching his own genitals. A child that touches his or her private parts habitually should not go unnoticed. "Parents can help children understand why these feelings are pleasurable and help them accept these feelings without becoming dependent upon them for emotional support. At this time of growth, 'harsh and hasty measures may make the child feel that his body and all of its functions are something to dread, rather than enjoy.' Parental fears and misconceptions about masturbation should not be allowed to create shame and disgust in the minds of young children about their normal exploration of the body and its parts."[1]

An interest in exploring his own body and the body of the opposite sex is not an indication of sexual perversion. He may only want to satisfy a God-given curiosity. A book for young children with appropriate pictures is one way to show and talk about body parts. This is not to say that parents are to allow young children to engage in "games" where body exposure is the purpose. These examinations should be discouraged but without creating feelings of guilt or shame.

Natural family settings need to be provided for your young child to see and learn about boy/girl body differences and to provide opportunities to observe the opposite sex. Of course, this works best if your family has children of the opposite sex. Bath time is a very natural setting for discussions about the differences between boys and girls. Changing clothes can also provide an opportunity to talk about differences.

With the awareness that boys have a penis and girls do not, some questions may develop about the differences in their bodies. The boy may wonder why he has a penis and the girl does not. The girl may also wonder why she does not have a penis.

These questions are real to the child and should not be taken lightly by the parent. This is a good time to use the book, *Boys and Girls— Alike and Different*, which has appropriate pictures for young children to help them understand that God made them different.

Attitudes about adult nudity in the home vary greatly from house to house. Up to about age three, your child may not really notice those natural times when you are nude. The younger preschooler does not think anything about your bathing or taking care of body eliminations. This is not to suggest that you parade around the house naked, though. Constant exposure to the adult nude body may create some anxious sexual feelings and unhealthy situations.

Around five or six your child will begin to show personal signs of modesty. He may want to be alone in his bedroom or in the bathroom. The parents' respect for his privacy will help to teach him to respect the privacy and modesty of other family members. On the extreme, you should not be overly concerned with modesty. If he casually comes in while a parent is undressed or in the bathroom, it is best to be relaxed about his presence. Helping him leave gracefully and without shame is also important. It will help him to have a relaxed acceptance of his own body.

Young children ask many questions. Some of these questions are about their bodies and babies. They will ask a parent anything. They are not yet embarrassed by any question. When questions come, it is wise to try to determine the source of the question.

When your child has a question that appears to you to be about her body or birth, first try to find out what she is thinking. Then answer her question as simply as possible. Be truthful. Be straightforward and at ease as you answer. Every bit of information you give is the foundation for future knowledge. If the foundation is false, the result will be distrust of parental information.

Young children are not interested in sitting down and discussing topics related to sex. Your child is more teachable and ready to learn when the subject comes up naturally.

A mother was bathing her two young children together. The older child was a boy and the other child a girl. The girl wanted to know why she did not have a penis. Since this was not the first time the two had bathed together, the mother realized that the girl had noticed a difference between herself and her brother.

Responding as naturally and calmly as possible, the mother said that boys have a penis and girls do not. The child still was not satisfied. The mother then realized that her daughter needed a special "name," too. When she told the child that girls have a vagina, the child was satisfied. Using the correct name for body parts is important. We help the baby learn the right name for his hands, eyes, feet, legs, fingers, and toes. But we seem to be embarrassed to call his penis what it is. Pet names for genitals may convey to the child that something is wrong with those parts of the body. Your child needs to learn from you, not her peers, what her genitals are called. Peer information tends to be incorrect and misleading.

When discussion of genitals and babies is treated as an unmentionable subject, the subject is glamorized. It's the "forbidden fruit" lure. If mom and dad cannot talk about it, it must be worse than four-letter words. Four-letter words are off limits, but they hold an attraction. By not teaching preschoolers the correct names for genitals and by not talking about the beginning of babies, these topics become something to snicker and giggle about with friends.

On the other hand, when the child is taught the correct names for genitals, and the subject of babies is calmly discussed and questions answered, the glamour of the topics disappears. The child simply learns to treat it matter-of-factly, as well as learning that these topics are to be discussed with mom and dad.

As with body modesty, you will begin to have opportunities to help your young child learn that certain subjects are to be discussed in private. Never convey that the subject is off limits, only that it is not to be talked about in public.

For example, I was in the grocery store with my four-year-old. He was sitting in the seat of the shopping cart. I had walked back about ten feet to pick up something I had passed. As I reached for the forgotten item, I heard him say in a normal speaking voice, "My penis itches." Before I could get back to the cart, he said it again.

When I reached the cart, I calmly placed the retrieved item in the basket and acknowledged that I had heard him. Without scolding him, I simply told him that we should only talk about his penis when we were at home. When we were out of our house, he should tell me quietly if he had a problem.

Just telling children once about what is private conversation is not enough. They simply do not learn what to do from one "telling." As with any other learned behavior, it takes time to help them know when it is appropriate to talk about their genitals.

These early years are the time to establish that mom and dad are neat people with whom to talk, and that mom and dad will talk to me about anything. If you wait until school age to talk about sex and the physical changes, your child may not listen, and she may not want to talk. You might even have lost your credibility. You were not interested before, why should she believe you are really interested now? Look for opportunities **now** to talk to your young child and be ready to listen.

What Am I Supposed to Say?

What you say comes in two forms—the words you actually speak and your actions. Both your words and your actions are guided by your own self-esteem. How you feel about yourself is reflected in your attitude toward the sex education of your children. You might want to reread "Knowing Who You Are as a Parent."

What children see being modeled in the home can shape their feelings and attitudes about sex and sexuality. When parents show love and respect for each other, the child learns to feel safe in showing and receiving love.

Parents who can lovingly touch and hold their children are providing sex education. Those children are learning that they are persons of worth. They have value and are important to someone—not because of what they can do, or how they look, but because of who they are.

The young child needs the love that touch conveys. Hold your child in your lap as you read books together. Be free to hug your child. Hold hands, not just when safety demands it, but as an expression that you are glad to be with your child.

Allow your child to express his love for you by hugging. He still may need to hug and kiss you before you leave the house. Do not take this gesture lightly. He needs to learn how to express his feelings to others that he loves. So that as an adult, he can express his feelings appropriately in a marital relationship.

Either parent can and should talk with either sex child about his or her body and the origin of babies. It is good, though, to be able to say, "Let's ask Mom/Dad if there is something else she/he can tell us," or "I do not know how to answer that question, but I will find out what you want to know." This second statement is not a put-off. You must get an answer and respond to your child.

So, what are you supposed to say? The following possible questions and answers may be of help to you as you and your child read *Boys and Girls—Alike and Different*. You can learn how to talk to your young child about his developing body and deal with his growing awareness that babies have a special beginning. These are not the **only** questions your child might ask, only a representation of possibilities. Your child may not ask any of these questions. You can be sure your child will ask uniquely phrased questions.

Do not feel that you must memorize the answers. These are designed only to familiarize you with what can be said. Once you get a feel for what to say, you will be more comfortable talking with your child.

"What's that?" (girl pointing to penis)
That's a penis.

"Is my penis inside of me?" (girl)
No. Girls do not have a penis.

"Why don't I have a penis?"
Because God planned for boys to have a penis. Boys and girls are different.

"What's a penis for?"
Boys urinate through the penis.

"Where do girls urinate?"
Girls urinate through a special place called the vulva.

"Did I once have a penis?" (girl)
No. Girls do not have a penis. Only boys have a penis.

"Will my penis ever come off?" (boy)
No. Your penis will always be a part of you.

"Can Beth touch my penis?"
No. Your body belongs to you. Your penis is private. No one should touch you there except your doctor, mom (dad), or me. We will only need to touch your penis if you are sick or have hurt yourself. You should not touch another boy's penis. You should not touch a girl's breasts, bottom, or vagina. Those are private parts.

"Can Peter touch my bottom?" (girl)
No. Your body belongs to you. Your bottom, vagina, and breasts are private. No one should touch you there except your doctor, dad (mom), or me. We will only need to touch your bottom, vagina, or breasts if you are sick or have hurt yourself. You should not touch another girl's breasts, bottom, or vagina. You should not touch a boy's penis or bot-

tom. Those are private parts.

"Is Mrs. Green's baby growing in her stomach?"
No. The stomach is where our food goes when we eat. God planned for a baby to grow in a special place inside the mother. That special place is called the uterus or womb.

"What does the uterus look like?"
The uterus looks like a balloon that has a little air in it. God planned for the uterus to stretch as the baby gets bigger.

"How did the baby get inside Mrs. Green?"
God planned for a small part of the daddy, called sperm, and a small part of the mother, called the egg, to start a baby.

"Where are the sperm?"
The sperm are in the scrotum of the daddy. The scrotum is the little bag or sack that hangs down behind the penis.

"Where is the egg?"
A mother's eggs are in a special place close to the uterus. The grown-up name for that special place is ovary.

"How does a baby eat inside the mother?"
God planned a special way for a baby to eat and get air. There is a tube, called a cord, that goes from the middle of the baby's tummy to the side of the uterus. Food and air from the mother's body go through that cord to the baby.

"Does the baby need the cord after it is born?"
No. The baby does not need the cord after it is born. The baby can eat and breathe by itself.

"Why do I have a belly button?"
Because that is where your cord was attached. The grown-up name for belly button is navel.

"How long does a baby grow inside the mother?"
A baby grows for nine months. That is about how long it will take you to go through kindergarten.

"What does the baby in Mrs. Watson look like now?"
Let me get a book that has pictures of a baby while it is still growing in the mother.

"Does it hurt to have a baby inside you?"
No. But sometimes the mother gets uncomfortable or tired.

"Can a mother feel the baby inside her?"
Yes. When the baby gets bigger, the mother can feel the baby move. Sometimes you can put your hand on the mother's tummy and feel the baby move.

"How does the baby come out?"
The baby comes out head first through the mother's vagina.

"How does a baby know when it is time to be born?"
God knows when it is time and prepares the mother for that time.

"Why did Peggy's mother go to the hospital to get her baby?"
Peggy's mother did not go to the hospital to get her baby. Her baby has been growing inside her uterus for nine months. Peggy's mother went to the hospital so a doctor could help her baby be born.

Situations Parents Face

There are so many different situations parents may face that they may find anticipating all of them impossible. As with the questions and answers, this section will present a variety of circumstances. Once you understand how to respond to a few situations, you should feel more at ease on other occasions.

You need to learn to be calm and at ease as you talk with your child. A young child is sensitive and can detect when you are uncomfortable. When he realizes that you are ill at ease talking about his body and answering questions about the source of babies, he may stop asking— not because he is embarrassed, but in an attempt to protect you from the awkward situation.

If you are in this position, get yourself back on track. You are the one who needs to be supplying this information to your child. Do not solely depend on your school (later) or your church. Your child needs to know you are knowledgeable about such things and available to answer his questions. One way to get back in touch with your child is to ask him a question about his body or the beginning of babies. That will let you know what information he has about a topic and will convey to him that you are willing to talk about the subject.

For example, you and your child are in the grocery store. During your time there you see a friend who is pregnant. Quietly say, "Mrs. Brown is going to have a baby." When in the car, you could ask any one of a number of questions. Your sole purpose here is to establish the fact that you are willing to talk about the beginning of babies. Possible questions: "Where do you think a baby grows inside a mother?" "How did we know Mrs. Brown was pregnant?" "Do we know any other women who are pregnant?"

Wait for his answer. Then respond as his answer dictates. The section with questions and answers may be helpful in preparing you to talk with your child.

Until your young child becomes comfortable asking you questions, use the above technique to reinforce the fact that you are willing to discuss the topic of babies. Watch for natural times to initiate the conversation.

Springtime has the potential for many natural situations. Baby birds are everywhere. A trip to the zoo would result in seeing many baby animals. A pet cat or dog, having a litter, would provide a perfect opportunity to talk about babies. Whatever you do to reopen communication with your preschooler, you need to become a person your young child can talk to about herself and the origin of babies.

Situations

What situations might you face as you live with a young child? The situations described here are by no means an exhaustive collection. The situations that follow are only a few of the ones you might possibly face.

Do not memorize these responses. You need to become familiar enough with what to say and how to react so that you can transfer these words and actions to other situations. Your goal should be to become comfortable, relaxed, and approachable. To borrow a phrase from today's slang, you need to be "the main man" in your young child's growing awareness of self and others.

Situation: You notice your young child touching his penis (her clitoris) while your family is watching television.

At a convenient break in the program ask your son (or daughter) to go to another room with you. Do not leave the impression that this sibling is being punished. Try to handle this conversation as discreetly as possible. You might say, "I noticed you were scratching your penis (clitoris). Do you have an itch, or do you need to urinate?" If he (she) says he (she) itches, help him (her) to understand that he (she) needs to be in a private place when he (she) scratches his penis (her clitoris). You may need to check for a rash or other problem. One parent discovered his son had a tick on his penis.

Situation: Your young child is your first child. She begins asking when she is going to get a baby sister.

"We would like to have another baby. Sometimes parents can only have one. I am so glad that God gave you to us. I am glad that you are a part of our family." Again, feel free to hug your child. Make sure she knows that you are glad to have her. Leave the door open to have this conversation again.

Situation: Your young child, of the opposite sex, comes into the bathroom while you are eliminating bodily waste or into the bedroom while you are dressing.

Remember that your child probably will not be embarrassed or think anything about being in the bathroom at this moment. You could say, "Daniel, I need to be alone for few minutes. Please close the door as you leave the bathroom. If you will go choose a book (game, toy, etc.), I will come to your bedroom to enjoy it with you." There are times when he simply wants to know where you are and what you are doing. A short explanation will expedite his departure. To avoid an unexpected visit, you may need to lock the bathroom door. Understand that when you lock the bathroom door, you have just introduced something he will try the next time he is in the bathroom alone. This is why it is good to teach that a closed door means the person inside wants to be alone. Therefore, you do not just walk into the room. Teach him to knock and respond to the answer given: "Come in," or "I will be out soon."

Situation: You discover your young child and one or more friends in her bedroom nude. It is obvious when you come in that they are exploring the differences of their bodies.

As startled as you may be, it is extremely important for you not to act startled or act hastily. In a soft and composed voice you might say, "I know boys and girls your age are curious about how bodies are different. I cannot allow you to explore each other. Your body is private. Put your clothes on." Involve the children in another activity. You may want to share the incident with the other parents.

Situation: You are breast-feeding your newborn. Your young child wants to know what the baby is doing to you.

You might say: "I am (Mom is) feeding our baby. In my (her) breast is milk for the baby. God planned this special way for a mother to feed her baby. Before the baby was born, my (her) breasts were changing."
How does the milk get in your (Mom's) breast?
God planned for a mother's breasts to have milk in them after a baby is born.
How does the milk come out?
Our baby is sucking on my (Mom's) breast like he would a bottle.

Situation: Your child tells you that an adult touched him on his penis and bottom.

Needless to say, the very thought of child sexual abuse can send your blood pressure up 100 points, not to mention the possibility of your child being abused. It is vital that you not go into a rage or show other strong emotions when your child begins to tell you about being touched.

As calmly as possible, encourage your child to tell you what happened. Let him do the talking. Do not put words into his mouth. Find out as much as you can about the circumstances surrounding the incident— where it happened, how long ago it occurred, and who the abuser is.

Comfort your child. Praise him for telling you what happened and say that telling you was the right thing to do. Explain to him that he will not be harmed for telling what happened. (The abuser may have told your child that he would hurt him if he told or that you would punish him if he told.)

Make every effort to alleviate your child's feelings of guilt or blame. These feelings are normal and should be acknowledged, but the abuser is the one who should feel guilty and is the one to blame!

You need to do several things once your child has told you about sexual abuse. Believe your child. Take your child to receive medical attention. This could be your own doctor or the hospital emergency room. Report the incident to the police. Sexual abusers must be stopped. Then be willing to seek professional counseling. You, your child, and the family will need help coping with the abuse.

Situation: You only suspect that your child has been sexually abused. How do you find out without putting words into your child's mouth and how do you approach your child?

Set the stage for your child to approach you. You might casually say: "Carlos, I read an article in my magazine about a little boy who had been touched by an adult on his penis and bottom. That little boy was afraid to tell anyone what had happened. He did not know that he would not get in trouble. He did not know that his parents would believe him and help him. Carlos, if anyone tries to touch or does touch you, I want you to tell me or Dad (Mom) about it. The person who does this to you needs help."

This impersonal and nonthreatening situation may open a flood-gate in your child. Now, be prepared to listen.

Other Situations

In addition to the above mentioned situations, there are other special concerns because of unique family makeups. One area of need might be the **single parent** who cannot be the role model of the opposite sex. This is where it is important to be active in a church. The child living in a single-parent home can be exposed to good role models because of friendships at church. Have men, as well as women, teach in the preschool areas at church. Preschool departments provide a natural setting for role models.

There may be families in your church who are available to host your child in their home or on an outing. Senior adults may be interested in being "grandparents" to her; young adults may be willing to become an "aunt" or "uncle." Seek out these special relationships. Sometimes people do not step forward because they do not know of the need.

Another situation is the **blended family**. Your older preschooler is in a blended family. Your wife died. Your family now consists of you and two children. You marry a woman whose husband has died. Your new wife has one child. Now your family has a mom, dad, and three children. Adjusting to the new parent and siblings is sometimes difficult. It is important that you and your wife work to help blend this family. This process may take some time to accomplish.

Helping the people who live in the same house feel like one family is a challenge. Meet the challenge. The children need both parents involved in their development. Being open to discussions about their body and the creation of babies is as important in this family setting as in the traditional family.

Another area of concern is **child abuse**: How to help a child avoid it; if the child has been abused, how to encourage the child to talk about it with a trusted person; and, what parents should do if their child is abused.

There are several myths about child abuse that parents need to know. The following are not necessarily all the myths, but probably the most common.[2]

- **Myth: Sexual abusers are usually strangers to their victims.** In nine out of ten cases, assailants are known by their victims. Sexual abusers can be primary caretakers, other relatives, neighbors, teachers, and professionals who work with children.

- **Myth: Incidents of child sexual abuse are always reported to the police.** Few incidents are reported. Actual figures are difficult to obtain. However, in cases of adult rape, conservative FBI estimates indicate that one out of three rapes is reported. If the abuser is a relative of a child victim, it is even less likely that the incident will be reported.

- **Myth: Sexual abuse of children is usually violent, and physical trauma is the greatest harm resulting from this kind of abuse.** Violent attacks and forced penetration of the victim occurs in only 5 percent of reported cases. The abuser often finds it easy to trick a child into sexual contact. Bribes and affection are the most effective tools of the sexual abuser. Psychological and emotional harm is the most devastating effect of sexual abuse of children.

- **Myth: Children make up stories about being sexually abused.** It is very rare that a child lies about sexual abuse. Often children have been told by their abusers that no one will believe their story. Therefore, children need support and comfort when they disclose what has happened to them. They need to be reassured that they are believed and that someone will help them.

- **Myth: Some children act seductively and want to have sexual relations with adults.** Children never ask to be sexually abused. While some children may be looking for affection or responding to it, the responsibility rests with the offender, not the victim. This also applies to cases where the abuser is someone the child knows or even loves.

- **Myth: Children never get over the harm of sexual abuse.** In cases where violent physical harm did not occur and where the assailant does not have a close relationship with the victim, children recover faster than adult victims. The most important factor in children's recovery is how appropriately the incident is handled by the adults who surround them.

A sexual abuser may try any or a combination of at least eight ways to get a child to cooperate.

1. Games Games are invented that involve sexual contact. The child is then convinced that the game is fun and that she will like playing it.

2. Friendship By being friendly to the child, the abuser can bring the friendship to the point that the child trusts the abuser and is expected to do what is asked.

3. Force The sexual abuser simply overpowers the child and forces her to cooperate.

4. Bribes The child is either promised or given gifts (or something else) appealing to the child in return for cooperation.

5. Withholding When the abuser is responsible for the care of the child, the abuser can effortlessly withhold what the child needs or wants.

6. Threats The child is told that the abuser will get them into trouble or will hurt her if she does not do what is requested.

7. Intimidation A child is easily led to believe that he is inferior, helpless, or weak. Once this is accomplished, he feels like he has to do what the abuser says.

8. Tricks A sexual abuser will lure a child into being alone with him or lead her to believe it is acceptable for her to do what the abuser asks.[3]

Protecting your young child, without creating unhealthy fear or alarm, is the challenge. It compares to teaching him not to play in the street, not playing with matches or fire, being careful in a parking lot, and not crossing a street alone. Keeping him safe is the goal, not making him paranoid.

Teaching your child not to respond aggressively against an attack seems to have more benefits than teaching her to defend herself. By keeping the sexual attack nonbrutal, she has a better chance of not being injured or killed. Often, if she can just say no and then run away, that can stop the assault. Because your child cannot know if the abuser is armed, remaining calm can prevent the attacker from instinctively pulling a possible hidden weapon. Conversely, if your child completes a self-defense course, this can produce a false sense of safety. A child who thinks she can fend off anyone may be less cautious than an untrained (but educated) child.

Teaching your young child to be safe is another deterrent of sexual abuse. There are three prominent ways to help him avoid a possible assault.

1. Avoid strangers. Do not talk to them unless a parent is present. Do not be alone with them. Do not accept candy, toys, or a ride from them unless a parent approves. Do not play with them unless you are given permission by a parent.

2. Stay away from people you think want to touch you. The above suggestions apply here also.

3. Learn to say NO! Your words and your actions can say NO! Some words might be: "NO! Don't touch me. I don't like it." "Don't do that." "I don't want to." Some actions that say NO! might be: running away, yelling, or screaming.

But suppose the unthinkable happens—your child is sexually abused. How should you respond and what should you do? Think of your child first. The abused child needs you on his side. Uncontrolled reactions (anger, disbelief, horror) can cause him to think these feelings are directed at him and not the abuser. Remember: Hindsight is twenty-twenty. Do not say "if only" or "what if I (the parent) had" in your child's hearing. Neither you nor your child is to blame. The attacker is at fault.

Do not be embarrassed to seek professional help for your child and your family. The abused child needs medical attention and counseling. Your family may also need counseling in order to quickly and healthily recover from the trauma that has occurred. The local rape crisis center is a good source for help.

Report the sexual abuse to the police. You are under legal obligation to report even suspected sexual abuse of a child. Also, your child is probably neither the first nor the last victim of the abuser. The abuser must be stopped.

Notes
[1]John C. Howell, *Teaching Your Children About Sex* (Nashville: Broadman Press, 1973), 51.
[2]Joy Berry, *Alerting Kids to the Danger of Sexual Abuse* (Waco, Texas: Word, 1984), inside back cover.
[3]*Ibid.*, 18-26.

Just for Parents of Middle-Aged Children

Norma Stevens

As parents, you are concerned that your middle-aged children will be mature, responsible Christians who apply biblical principles to their everyday living. You want your children to be educated about sexuality and how God intends for sexuality to be expressed. You want your children to acquire a good measure of self-esteem and self-discipline and not to become sexually active before adulthood and marriage. That's why you are reading this book and hopefully will be leading your children to read the book in this series, *My Body and Me*, written for them.

For anyone, male or female, adult or child, the acceptance of one's self and the appreciation of who he is, is essential to being able to achieve his potential. You can best help your child by having an appreciation for who you are, by accepting that you are made in God's image and are special in His sight.

You can then guide your child in understanding how special he is to God. A child needs to understand the wonder of God's design of the human body. He needs to learn how each part of the body works and to see that he is the product of an awesome and wonderful Creator.

When children are helped to understand how their bodies work, they can begin to understand a little of what God created. The human body is an amazingly complex machine composed of more than fifty million microscopic cells which make up tissue, muscles, blood, and organs. When children begin to realize that no man-made machine can even come close to what the human body is capable of, they can better appreciate how special they are.

Middle-aged children need to be taught about the digestive system, the body's mechanism for sustenance, for absorbing nourishment; about the respiratory system which deals with the air we breathe to supply oxygen to the body and to dispose of carbon dioxide; about the circulatory system which consists of miles of tubes carrying blood to all parts of the body with oxygen and nutrients and then absorbing waste materials; about the urinary system which rids the body of the waste materials collected by the circulatory system.

Middle-aged children need to be taught about the control systems of the body: the nervous system and the endocrine system and how each works. The endocrine system operates through hormones produced by glands. Discussing this system provides a convenient way to lead to a discussion of the reproductive system as the hormones regulate the body's development including growth and sexual maturity. Sex education is a natural link to understanding about how the body works and it should always be taught in light of how special we are to God.

From all of this knowledge and awareness can come a sense of worth. Without this sense of worth, a child has little or no respect for his body or for the bodies of other people. It is the person who judges

What It Means to Become a Christian

Parents, God has given you the responsibility of guiding your children's spiritual growth. In order to best accomplish this task, your own personal and genuine salvation experience is important. If you have not accepted Jesus Christ as your personal Savior or if you need to refresh your memory about what the Bible says about how to be born again, read and study the following Bible verses. This plan of salvation will be valuable as you answer your child's questions and lead him or her to become a Christian.

1. "For all have sinned, and come short of the glory of God" (Rom. 3:23). Everyone is a sinner; there are no exceptions.
2. "For the wages of sin is death; but the gift of God is eternal life through Jesus Christ our Lord" (Rom. 6:23). Death means separation forever from God and His love through Jesus Christ.
3. "But God commendeth his love toward us, in that, while we were yet sinners, Christ died for us" (Rom. 5:8). God loves us sinners so much that He gave His son to die for our sins.
4. "If thou shalt confess with thy mouth the Lord Jesus, and shalt believe in thine heart that God hath raised him from the dead, thou shalt be saved" (Rom. 10:9). To be born again, you must believe that Jesus died for your sins and state publicly that you accept Him as Lord of your life.
5. "For whosoever shall call upon the name of the Lord shall be saved" (Rom. 10:13). This is God's promise to you that if you accept Jesus as Lord, He will accept you.

After having read and studied these verses, you may have additional questions about what it means to become a Christian. If so, contact a Christian friend or a minister. They will be happy to answer your questions and pray with you and your family that you may come to know Jesus Christ as your personal Lord and Savior.

himself or herself to be worthless who will treat sex as a means of self-gratification, something to be gotten at whatever cost.

A child needs to know that, in God's wondrous plan, He made two different kinds of bodies for people—male and female—and that He designed the bodies so that each has a special part to play in having babies in married love.

Middle-aged children need to begin to understand that sex for the sake of self-enjoyment alone denies the purposes for which God created it. God's purposes include the ongoing of the human race and the deepest, most intimate way a husband and wife have of expressing their love for each other. They need to realize that a wonderful dimension of marriage would be missing if two people, set apart for each other through the covenant of marriage, had no different expression for their love than that used between parent and child or between friends. Sex is a sacred dimension because it is ordained by God.

What middle-aged children need from parents in sex education at this point in life is to:

1. Receive accurate, factual, reliable information without a sermon accompanying each bit of information;

2. Be a part of ongoing discussions about sex that originate both from the child and from the adult arising naturally from things happening in their lives (taking trips to a farm or zoo, their pet giving birth, a new baby being born in the family);

3. Learn attitudes and values through parental role modeling and through discussions of why people do what they do and what the Bible teaches.

Johnny needs to be taught and retaught that he is unique, that he is special, that God loves him and wants the best for him. Susie needs to be told there is no one else like her in the world, and that God meant for it to be that way, and God knows and cares about her down to the last hair on her head. Every child needs to be taught that because he is special it does not give him license to act any way he wants to; that his specialness carries with it a lot of responsibility.

Children have to learn all of these things gradually. They can be led through Bible study, observing the world around them, and through honest and open discussions with you, their parents.

A Look at Middle Childhood

Your child is growing and changing everyday in so many ways. This period of time, usually defined as eight and nine years of age, is the dividing line between early childhood and preadolescence. Your child is growing steadily but more slowly than in the past. The large muscles are still developing, as are the small muscles. Your child is becoming more coordinated and can participate in activities involving detailed work. His or her eyes are more able to do close work than in the previous years so that reading is more pleasurable both physically and intellectually.

Your child is probably full of energy and does not tire easily although his heart is developing more slowly and he may experience periods of fatigue. For some children, permanent teeth are still appearing. Vocal cords and lungs are developing more rapidly and children of this age enjoy using both to their fullest. The onset of puberty begins during these years and some children will reach puberty in their ninth year. Because of this physical maturing, your child needs to be taught about his body and how it functions.

Since your middle-aged child is on the dividing line of growth and maturity, you need to realize there is a pull toward independence at the same time that she needs the security of home and family. She is no longer a small child. Even her body may reflect this as it loses the roundness of babyhood and becomes more angular. Sometimes your child may appear to be wonderfully coordinated and the next moment display an unexpected clumsiness. She is having to get used to knees and elbows extending where they didn't before.

Both physically and emotionally, middle-aged children lose a certain kind of innocence as they become conscious of their bodies. Like Adam and Eve in the garden, they no longer can be unaware of their naked- ness. They need privacy, even though they may not always realize that the same is true for others as well.

Children this age want to be good because they want to please parents and God. The child is becoming aware of the two opposing forces of good and bad. He is interested in heaven and has a lot of questions about God. For these reasons, and under the guidance of the Holy Spirit, a middle- aged child often makes a confession of faith and accepts Jesus as Savior.

Your middle-aged child is conscious of right and wrong even if she doesn't always make appropriate decisions. She is more comfortable with rules and regulations, especially if she can participate in estab- lishing them, than in discussing why a person should or should not do certain things. Laws, religious or civil, are important to middle-aged children. Because of this belief in the law, which may change as she gets older, this is a crucial time for serious teaching of biblical, Christian principles concerning moral responsibility in sex.

Your child probably enjoys organized group activities and games, but you cannot expect her to assume too much responsibility just yet. She enjoys being given definite responsibilities but may become discour- aged if you exert too much pressure to do too many things.

Your middle child's world is expanding and encompasses people you don't know—other children, their parents, school workers, even people in your neighborhood. Because your child's world is expanding, it is crucial by this age, to have given him enough knowledge to prevent him from becoming a victim of sexual abuse. (See the material at the end of the section, "Just for Parents of Young Children.")

Outside influences are on the rise and competing with your influence on your child. Your child is concerned about himself and is beginning the lifelong practice of self-appraisal. He may be capable of independent thinking but often be uncertain about his choices and decisions. He needs encouragement, acceptance, and praise from you and other adults as he is often supersensitive to criticism. Peers become important to the middle-aged child. He is better able to cooperate and to work in groups and this ability means he has a strong interest in clubs and groups of the same sex. This is the age of hero worship and love of folklore and myths.

Boys generally become exceedingly disdainful of girls. Girls don't usually exhibit such strong negative feelings about boys and your daughter may even feel rejected when favorite playmates don't want to bother with her. Also, at about age eight, children begin to become aware of the opposite sex in different ways than before. This new awareness may account for their seeming disdain and rejection of the opposite sex since this kind of interest is somewhat frightening to the child.

Children learn a lot about sex from same-sex friends, much of which is incorrect or garbled. As children use a child's logic and combine that with misinformation, the results may well be wildly off-target. For example, many children believe the doctor brings the baby to mother in the hospital. One day, an "enlightened" peer tells an eight- or nine-year-old friend that isn't the way it happens at all and proceeds to share his or her version of conception.

Some children think the navel is where the father puts his penis during intercourse, or that the navel is where the baby comes out. Others believe mothers swallow some kind of seed that grows in their stomachs. Such concepts may not be as out of touch as the old stork tales and cabbage patch stories. They do, however, alert us to the fact that when children become aware of babies and wonder where they come from, they begin to build their own constructs of beliefs based on the knowledge (well-founded or unfounded) they already have.

You can help your middle-aged child learn the facts by answering questions as she asks them. The section that follows, "Questions You Might Be Asked," will provide you assistance in responding appropriately. You may help the process by opening conversations when appropriate occasions arise.

Children enjoy ridiculous kinds of humor and can usually find something to laugh about in almost any situation. They have a growing appreciation for imaginary adventure. One of the ways children at this age learn about their world comes out of their natural curiosity. Facts are fascinating to them, but so is fiction. They will always carry things beyond the known to the imaginary, writing new scripts as they go.

They are rather indiscriminately interested in anything new and their curiosity is at an all time peak. Eight- and nine-year-olds are alert to their environment and notice a lot of things they did not notice earlier. Even passages in the Bible which they did not question before come under scrutiny. The birth of Jesus, for example, may raise questions or comments which need clarifying.

Relating to Middle-Aged Children

How do you relate to where your child is physically, spiritually, intellectually, emotionally, and socially at this age? Some gradual changes in parenting need to take place as the child matures. As you experience your child's growth, your own self-image begins a subtle reorganization. You have had a picture in your mind as being the parent of a small child which is no longer true. Your child may be almost as tall as you if you happen to be short. This is a youngster who no longer fits comfortably and snugly into your lap, although there will still be times when he or she, seeking comfort, will try to do just that. Perhaps your formerly soft, pink-cheeked little girl seems to be disheveled and a bit grubby most of the time. Maybe your handsome little boy seems to be all bruises and scratched legs and have a bottomless stomach as he eats everything in sight. He is not the same child he was when he was five years old and it is inappropriate to treat him the same way.

As has been indicated, some children reach puberty at this age. Even if they do not, they are in the beginning stage of development which culminates in puberty. A girl of nine may begin her menstrual periods and be within the normal range of development. Both sexes perspire and may have a slight body odor. Both boys and girls may masturbate. It will probably seem to you, as a parent, that these changes have happened sooner than you had anticipated and you may not feel ready to deal with a teenager in a child's body. Of course, your child may be a late bloomer, but it is still better to be prepared.

A middle-aged child is a complex blend of small child and budding adolescent. As such, this is the time when he or she needs you to be able to read all of the signs (words, body language, and circumstances), and to make responses and decisions which are appropriate and understandable.

While you may have thought nothing of walking in on a five- or six-year-old while he or she is bathing, this is not acceptable to a child of eight- or nine-years-old. Privacy may become almost a life or death matter. An eight-year-old may not even want to change clothes in front of you and will be embarrassed if you persist in invading his or her private life space.

As parents, we need to remember that children should not be compared with siblings, with the neighbor's children, or those of a relative. Each child is unique and has been programmed genetically to develop and mature in certain ways at certain times. Your child will have some of the same characteristics of his or her mother, father, grandparents, but all of these characteristics are put together in a configuration different from that of anyone else in the world. For that reason, your child may or may not follow the usual patterns of maturing. There are other reasons which may alter the pattern set genetically such as sickness or malnutrition.

A good self-concept and a positive attitude toward one's self-worth is vital for optimum growth. Children develop desirable traits by the way other people react to them, especially their parents. If your child judges himself negatively, due to early or late maturation, it will be difficult to dissuade him from his ideas unless he has been prepared for such eventualities. Without sensitive guidance, sexual maturing can be a traumatic time in the life of a child.

Even as children are developing physically, so are they developing emotionally and socially. If a nine-year-old is encouraged to take a leadership role at school, it may be difficult for him or her to always be in the followship role at home. You must be able to relate to the multi-dimensional person your child is becoming.

At the same time, you must try to understand the difficulty of remembering all the rules of social conduct. The same little boy who is elected hall monitor may not always think at the dinner table to ask that something be passed rather than reaching across the table for it. How can such responsibility be evident in one case and not the other? Quite easily! New, out-of-the-ordinary things will elicit correct responses while older rules and regulations often get lost in the forest of social interaction.

If a boy this age categorically rejects all girls, including his sisters, little is accomplished by insisting that he play with girls regardless of how he feels. This stage will pass all too soon. Remember your child is experiencing strong feelings associated with sexual differences and with the move toward individualization and independence. On the other hand, many children relate well with those of the opposite sex. They never seem to have problems with whether the other child is male or female as they work or play with him or her.

Your child is growing spiritually. Many Christian parents see their children profess faith in Christ as personal Savior. To relate to him or her as a brother or sister in Christ is often a new concept, bringing about new feelings. As you try to guide and direct your child as he matures in the Christian faith, his spiritual insights may bring a refreshing breeze into your own life. However, watching him attempt to balance his new-found faith and his lack of experience in the world may lead to deep concern on your part as you attempt to help him love everyone and yet be cautious about people, even those he knows and loves. He must learn a knowledgeable love, one based on the realization that not all humans will want what is best for him.

Questions You Might Be Asked

While some of these questions might surprise you, they are representative of ideas which puzzle middle-aged children, even if children do not have the precise vocabulary used in the questions. The answers given are only one way of responding to children of this age and are to be considered as general guidelines.

Remember the earlier suggestion about asking your child to explain what he or she understands or thinks is the answer. Then you can clarify, modify, or add to what is already known.

Questions from middle-aged children do not necessarily come in an orderly sequence. In addition, while you may answer a question in such a way that you think you have covered all of the factors, your child may ask something else a short time later that will require you to talk about the same idea from a different perspective. He or she may ask exactly the same question again.

"Where do babies come from?"

They come from their mothers. They grow from a tiny cell created by the coming together of the father's sperm and the mother's egg. When they become large enough, they are born.

"Where does the cell come from?"

The mother has a special part of her body which produces eggs. When one of the ovaries produce an egg cell or ovum, it can meet a sperm cell from the father.

"Where does it go after it joins together?"

The fertilized egg attaches itself to the uteran wall. The placenta develops as a result of implantation. There it will get everything it needs to live and to grow.

"Where do fathers grow sperm cells?"

They are formed in the testicles, that part of the man's body in the soft pouch underneath the penis.

"How does the baby get out when it gets big enough?"

Babies are born by coming out through the mother's vagina.

"Does it hurt when the baby comes out?"

The mother has to work hard to help the baby come out and it does hurt. But she most often has a lot of assistance from doctors and nurses.

"How can a baby eat and drink and go to the bathroom?"

When the fertilized egg attaches to the wall of the uterus, there is a cord-like tube that connects the baby to the mother so that when she eats and drinks, all of the food the baby needs to grow passes through the tube, called the umbilical cord. The part that the baby doesn't need would pass out of the mother's body as bowel movements or urine goes back through the mother's body and is processed through her kidneys and bladder.

"What does puberty mean?"

Puberty is the time when the bodies of boys and girls change and develop. These changes occur over several years, and people change at different rates. Some girls start these changes about nine years of age, others as late as sixteen or eighteen. Some boys might start at ten and others as late as seventeen. When girls begin to change, they often begin their menstrual periods. When boys begin to change, their voices deepen, and they begin growing hair on their bodies. (It might be well at this point to assure the child that you will explain any and every change that happens to him or to her and that you will be excited with your child about this evidence of growth.)

"At what age do boys start to shave?"

That depends on each boy's individual timetable. Boys usually look forward to being able to shave and may start earlier than they need to which is often as late as seventeen or eighteen.

"What is a sperm?"

It is a male sex cell which carries half of the genes necessary for the development of a baby. The sperm is made in the testicles and carried in the semen. Each sperm is tiny and has a tail to help it move through the woman's body toward an ovum. It looks a lot like a tadpole.

"Does a woman's eggs look like chicken eggs?"

Not exactly. They are much smaller and round but they do not have hard shells.

"When will my eggs be ready to make a baby?" (girl)

After you start your menstrual cycle, although it will be a long time before you are ready to care for a baby properly.

"Why does my penis look different from some of the other boys?" (boy)

Every boy develops in a way that is right for him and different from other boys in some ways. So your penis may be smaller or larger than theirs. Also, some boys may have been circumcised and others haven't been. When parents want a boy to be circumcised because of their religious or health beliefs, it usually is done in the hospital right after the baby is born. The flap of skin on the end of the penis, called the foreskin, is removed. So your penis may look different from others in this way.

"Can you get a baby if a boy puts his penis on you anywhere?" (girl)

No, a man must place his penis very close or in the woman's vagina so that the sperm can swim up the vagina to the uterus. Then a sperm must join with an egg before the baby starts to grow inside the woman.

"Why doesn't (names a couple) **have any children?"**

Some people don't have children because of medical problems such as infertility. This means that they don't produce eggs or sperm, or that something happens to keep conception from taking place. Some people don't have children for other reasons and these are usually personal. So it is a good idea not to ask a couple why they do not have any children.

"Why did (names a couple) **baby die?" Or "Why is the baby still in the hospital?"**

Sometimes a baby is born before it has grown enough to live or there is something wrong with one of its organs that the doctors can't fix. If the baby needs just a little more time to grow, often he or she stays in the hospital in a special kind of bassinet called an incubator that is as much like the mother's womb as is possible. Then when the baby gets strong enough, the baby can go home.

"How long does it take to grow a baby inside a woman?"

It takes about nine months.

"What's the curse?"

It's a slang term for menstruation and is usually used by people who don't understand the wonder of the reason for menstruation.

"Will it hurt when I start my period?" (girl)

Not usually. You may not even realize when you've started. The first time or two there may just be a brownish discharge from your vagina. Later on, if you should have some cramping, there are several things such as exercise that will help.

"Why do girls make such a secret about menstruating?"

Because it is something private and because children sometimes make jokes about it because they don't understand. It is perfectly normal and is a sign that the girl's body is maturing just as it should.

"How old will I be when I get hair 'down there'?"

You will get hair on and around your genitals when the hormones in your body send the signal. When that happens differs with people; some develop early and some late. It is another sign that your body is developing as it should.

"What exactly do you do when you make love?"

Remember that making love is something God designed for husbands and wives to show their love for each other. It is a special way of hugging and kissing just for a husband and wife. They lie very close together in bed. They tell each other how much they love the other one and then the man puts his penis into the woman's vagina. It is a very good feeling and it is the way the sperm enters the woman's body to start its long journey.

"The big kids were talking about 'making out.' What does that mean?"

It depends on how old they are and what they know. It might mean making love; it could mean a lot of hugging and kissing without sexual intercourse.

"Why does getting married make babies come?"

Because this is when a man and woman can follow God's plan. They can begin making love and this is the right time because they can prepare a home for a baby.

"What does contraceptive mean?"

Contraceptive is something that a married couple uses to keep the woman from getting pregnant. There are pills that a married woman can take or a device she can use to prevent conception from taking place. Or a married man might use a condom, a sheath (covering) that fits over the penis.

"How often do married people have intercourse?"

That depends on the couple. Some have intercourse every night; some only every week or so. They may be very busy or tired or not feel well and choose not to express their love for each other in this way every day. The wonderful thing about God's plan for married people is they have choices.

"Do you just know how to have intercourse when you get married or what?"

People don't have to be taught but some discussion with a doctor and a counselor is good to have before marriage so that each person can better understand the other one.

"When can I have intercourse?"

When you grow up, fall in love, and get married. Intercourse is a gift from God but it must be used in the right way at the right time. The right time is after you get married.

"Do you and daddy (or mama) **do it** (intercourse) **just because it feels good?"**

We often express our love for each other in this way and we enjoy it very much. We shouldn't think of intercourse as a game, but as a wonderful experience that carries with it a lot of responsibility.

"Can two men make love?"

There are men who only want to have sex with other men. The Bible tells us that this is wrong. We now know that men can get a very serious disease called AIDS when they have sex with each other.

"Can two women make love?"

The same thing is true for women as for men.

"Is it bad to be a homosexual?"

The Bible tells us that it is wrong to be sexually active with a person of the same sex. But we must care about a person even if we don't like what he or she does. Also a homosexual has the constant fear of contracting AIDS.

"Why do some people think it's OK to kiss on the cheek but not on the mouth?"

Kissing on the mouth is a very intimate thing and really should be done only by a man and woman who love each other. There are a lot of germs that can be spread in this way and even husbands and wives have to be careful when one of them has a cold or fever.

"If a lot of people have intercourse because it feels good, why does anyone get married?"

God said that intercourse is only to happen within marriage. Getting married says that you are committed to each other for the rest of your life. It declares to the world that you love each other and that you are two responsible people. If a baby comes as a result of intercourse within marriage, it will have a mother and a father to look after it.

"Can I get AIDS?"

Yes, unless you live by God's standards and are careful with medical procedures. The AIDS virus is transmitted through the exchange of infected body fluids. Many homosexuals and heterosexuals are infected with the virus through sexual involvement and promiscuity, but many others are infected through unscreened blood transfusions or through contaminated needles used for the injection of drugs. A mother who carries the virus can transfer it to her unborn child in the womb. You can get AIDS through any of these forms of transmission.

"What does 'P.G.' mean?"

"P.G." is one way of saying pregnant. It means that the woman is going to have a baby.

"Will a blind (deaf, lame) **person have a blind baby?"**

Not usually unless there is something in one of the genes which the baby inherits.

"What would make a deformed baby?"

Sometimes things can go wrong between conception and birth. If the mother drinks alcohol, abuses drugs, or smokes, this can happen, or if she has some serious diseases, or has an accident. Sometimes there is something wrong with the egg or sperm.

"What is a fetus?"

It is the baby in the mother's womb after about three months of growing; it is called an embryo up until that time.

"Can people have intercourse when the baby is growing inside the mother?"

Yes, if the mother's doctor says that everything is all right.

"Did you and Dad (or Mother) **have intercourse before I was born?"**

Yes. (Unless the child is referring to a stepparent or is an adopted child. In those cases, further explanation needs to be given.)

"Did I see you do it?"

No, you were growing high up in the womb, floating in the fluid surrounding you, with your eyes closed. Even if they had been open you could not have seen anything.

There are many, many other questions which children of this age will, and do, ask. However, in some cases, children exhibit no curiosity about human sexuality. A lack of verbalization does not mean a lack of interest but is probably indicative of embarrassment or fear or even the inability to put concerns into questions. When this has been the pattern in your child, you would do well to create an opportunity for questions to emerge naturally. For example, you might baby-sit a baby of the opposite sex of your child and have him help you care for the baby. You can bring up the subject of anatomical differences and say, "Maybe you've wondered about why boys and girls are different," and talk a little about sex differences with your child.

Again, children need enough information, understanding, and sense of values to protect them from sexual abuse and from games with peers which have the possibility of physical or psychological damage.

You, as a parent, have a responsibility and obligation to provide guidance and direction in sex education but it is also a privilege to be cherished.

Just for Parents of Preadolescents and Young Adolescents

Susan Lanford

"Caught in the middle!" "Never-never land!" Just who are and where are these preadolescent and young adolescent kids? The girl pestering you for eye shadow and lipstick may be the same girl who sleeps with her security blanket at night. The boy who insists that you not touch him in any way, shape, or form in public may be the same boy who plops on your lap to tell you the latest joke.

Growing Preadolescents

Preadolescents are caught between two developmental stages—childhood and adolescence. They move quite freely between these distinct stages, and they are rarely bothered by the inconsistencies which this journeying back and forth produces in their behavior or attitudes. As their parents, you and I occasionally trip up. We'll find ourselves saying within a short span: "Don't act like a little kid!" and "Stop trying to grow up so fast!" I suppose we're caught in *their* middle, too.

Luke 2:52, a familiar verse, reminds us that Jesus grew in every critical developmental area. He changed mentally, physically, socially, and spiritually. To know your preadolescent **and young adolescent**, realize that she is changing in these same ways as well.

Growing Mentally

This can be an exciting time for preadolescents. They are showing a mental capacity for more complicated tasks and for solving more complex problems. They have a reading vocabulary of 50,000 words and can use technical words, such as computer commands or scientific terminology.[1]

This expanded use of language does not mean that their way of thinking is much changed. They are in a stage of mental development known as *concrete operational*. To get from point A to point B, they need an immediate experience and information which makes sense to them. While much of their school experience is built on a "knowledge for knowledge's sake" foundation, they are better able to focus on and be interested in a topic which has some relevance in their world. They need a point of personal reference.

While their attention span is growing, they are more selective in using it. In other words, the same child who can play for hours with home video games may tune out his forty-minute English class each day from lack of interest.

Sex differences do not explain differences in their mental growth. Interestingly, however, there is some evidence that children who physically mature early have stronger verbal skills at this age. Those who are late maturing have better spatial and mathematical abilities.[2]

Take note: The early enthusiasm for school you see in your younger children quickly wears off. By fifth and sixth grades, easily 50 percent of school children dislike school.[3]

Their selective attention span explains a bit of this dislike. But we must not understate the social dimension of this shift regarding school. The "pack" gains the high ground. Peers are significant—not just their two or three good buddies but all their peers. Finding and keeping a place in the larger group of everyone in their grade in their school is important.

Shifts in school populations have propelled many "tweenagers" like projectiles away from childhood and toward adolescence. Many sixth graders are in middle school. My children's school system places fifth *and* sixth graders in middle school. Once displaced from elementary school, they turn their backs on some childhood likes and activities. Increasingly, they are drawn to the music, clothes, language, and leisure activities of the adolescent world just ahead of them.

Growing Physically

Much in the book for preadolescents, *Sex! What's That?*, is devoted to the physical changes they can expect. I hope you will read the second and third chapters now if you have not already. I won't repeat here what is said there.

The startling fact about their *physical* growth is that *so much* of it is prompted by hormonal secretions from their sex glands and the *sexual maturing* that their bodies undergo.

The good news for parents is that most preadolescents are still in the early, gradual phases of this sexual maturing process. But the urgency for us is this: to talk honestly with them about the changes on the way *before the full onslaught of adolescent hormones hits*. Once this storm is unleashed, the emotional ups and downs make talks about sexuality, morality, and behavior more difficult.

Am I saying talk now so that you won't have to talk during "teenagedom?" Certainly not. I *am* saying talk now so that talks in the stormy years which follow have precedents.

There is no soldier more thoroughly beaten and demoralized than the one caught in an ambush, not ready to do battle. I'm convinced it is an act of ultimate respect for your child to let him in on the secret that an adolescent "ambush" lies ahead. Equip him in the relative calm of these "tweenage" years for the storm, physically and emotionally speaking, of the teenage years.

Growing Socially

Our young adolescents are gaining social skills for more varied relationships. But the growing importance and influence of peers is one change we parents hesitate to celebrate.

Why? Despite the demands on us of raising children, it is difficult to move off the center of their world. You'll find the compliant child you shopped for wrangling over your choice of clothes, to the point of refusing to wear them. She's ready for a say in her wardrobe. Your absolute power begins to erode. This same child will regale you with details of hair bows, earrings, colors, and styles. She's watching her group, and beginning to form opinions from her observations of what is acceptable dress, speech, and behavior. Your less-than-absolute influence slips a notch or two.

What is going on? With a bit of objectivity we realize that they are feeling the first stirring of independence from parents. It is the major developmental feat they must accomplish through their adolescent years.

The importance of their peers will become even stronger as they grow into teenagers. You've already heard or noticed enough about their peers to give you pause, I'm sure. Let me suggest four ways we parents can positively respond to the reality of peer power on our children:

1. Realize that you now have, and will continue to have during their adolescence, a major impact on their lives.

2. Widen their circle of adults and reinforce the time they spend with adults who share your values and who practice an everyday-brand of Christianity.

3. Determine to know their friends and maintain on open-door policy at home to them.

4. Encourage them to bond to small groups that have a positive influence on them.

For the next ten or twelve years, you cannot fight a running battle with peer power and win. But you can help shape and mold their social growth in these four ways. If you remain unconvinced that this is important, realize that peers supply 90 percent of information on birth control and sexuality to today's teenagers.[4] And the statistics on teen pregnancy, AIDS cases, teenaged abused and abusers, clearly show this information to be inadequate, inaccurate, and lacking a Christian value system.

Growing Spiritually

Preadolescence is a time of significant spiritual growth opportunities. Much of this derives from their expanding mental capabilities. These kids can do more than listen to a Bible story and parrot it back. They can learn a Bible truth or a principle for living from a Bible passage or from a Bible character's life. They can apply the truth from the Bible to their own experiences.

Teaching these children is exciting. They are learning on a deeper level, using abstract reasoning at times. Yet they are not plagued with the doubts and skepticisms or plain disinterest that teenagers may exhibit at church or about spiritual matters.

In fact, the basic concepts of sin, redemption, and salvation are just now being grasped. I do not say this to cause you panic over the spiritual state of your child. Children who profess a personal faith in Jesus Christ at young ages have genuine experiences of salvation. As preadolescents, these same children will understand, as they could not before, some of the universality of sin. If your children are not Christians, this is an ideal age to talk frankly with them about this life-changing choice. (See "How to Become a Christian" in the section for parents of middle-aged children.) They have the mental capability and the spiritual curiosity to understand their need for redemption. They do not need to be pushed toward a profession of faith. But you can overtly pray for and with your preadolescent about becoming a Christian.

Sexuality in Our Children's World

One Wednesday night driving home from church, my children began telling me about a hot, new group coming to town for a concert. Then eight- and ten-year-olds, they filled me in on how the group members dressed, the songs they sang, on and on. Then they began to name the individuals. "Well, there's so and so, the one with the longest hair. And this one who sings on every song. And that one who's a homosexual... " Huh? I think I remained composed on the outside, and I think I did an admirable job of pulling my car out of a near collision with the guardrail. But on the inside, my heart was pounding. My mind was reeling with questions: "How did they learn that word? Do they know what it means? Is this a teachable moment? Shouldn't I start a calm, frank discussion here? Is this a big deal or not? If it's not, will I make it one by asking my kids about it? Do I . . . are they . . . should we . . . what if . . . ? At least they used the correct word and not some street word."

I finally managed to choose a course of action and inquired, oh so offhandedly, "Hmmm, I've never heard you use the word *homosexual* before; what does it mean?"

"Oh, you know, Mom, just that guys like only guys, and girls like only girls."

"Oh, OK, who taught you about this?"

"Oh Mom, everybody knows it; no one *taught* it to me."

I had one small window opened to me on the information stored in my children's minds. Like many tidbits of sexual information, this one was pointed in the general direction of accuracy, but a long way from it.

We finished the drive home. We talked more about the difference in guys *liking* guys, and guys being *sexually attracted to* guys, and the difference in how those two feelings are expressed. We talked about the truth that we are created either male or female and about God's design for those differences.

That fifteen-minute slice of life convinced me that simply knowing my child is not enough information for effectively parenting my child, especially in this critical area of sexuality. I must know the world he moves in and the information she's caught and taught, if I'm to be all the parent I can be—for *their* sakes.

I'd like to share a few examples of what sexuality is like in your child's world. As you read, you may wonder, "Why is she telling me about teenage behavior?" Two reasons: (1) you've almost got one in your home, and your child knows about and is curious about many aspects of a teenager's world; and (2) the boundaries separating the adult world from the childhood world are virtually gone. Speaking generally, there's little protection for your child from media images of adult themes and sexual scenes. Your constant vigilance, which I commend and encourage you to continue, is not a perfect filter.

Here's some of what's getting through to our children in their world.

Song Lyrics

Top-40 music regularly includes lyrics on sexual subjects. Most troubling is that these subjects are described in crude, explicit, detailed ways. Tipper Gore of the Parents Music Resource Center quotes Smokey Robinson who calls such lyrics "auditory pornography."[5] Add these lyrics to a live concert, with sensual costumes and sexually suggestive behavior on stage, and the sexual saturation is overwhelming, especially in young lives.

Not a preteen issue? Oh, but it is. Your child may not be at those live concerts, but many preteens are. It will be all the talk at school next day. *You* may not subscribe to MTV, but *some* household they visit will. You may only buy Christian tapes for the Walkman, but Top-40 radio is as near as the flick of a switch.

Mrs. Gore tells two other troubling impressions in her book, *Raising PG Kids in an X-Rated Society*: (1) Rock musicians and promoters are deliberately targeting the preteen fans, and (2) the ones creating musical mayhem, performers and producers, on sexual subjects are unconcerned (the Christian word would be *unrepentant*) about its impact on young fans and are aggressive about their rights to produce any music for any audience.[6]

Comingling of Sex with Violence

Certainly the media has promoted sex and violence. Researchers found that over 50 percent of music videos shown on MTV included or implied violence; 35 percent portrayed violence against women.[7] Again, in some rock lyrics, your child can hear that a penis is like a gun, knife, or sword, that a vagina is something to be cut or sliced, and that ejaculation is like shooting a gun where semen becomes the bullets.[8]

There is a film genre known as "teen slasher" movies where your child can see young lovers cut in pieces, death by castration, and explicit scenes of gang rape.[9] For your impressionable preteen or young teen, the mixing of sex with violence is a confusing, troubling message. But its greatest tragedy is that young minds—troubled, confused, even repulsed as they may be—will ingest these images as truth and use them to form some of their sexual attitudes in the years to come. When a Rhode Island Rape Crisis Center surveyed children, a majority said rape was *acceptable behavior.* Over a two-year period in the late '80's, arrests of *thirteen-year-old* boys for rape offenses increased *200 percent* in New York City.[10]

The so-called "soft" pornography of men's magazines sometimes sends the same convoluted message. In fact, one study particularly examined the visual images of children in *Playboy, Hustler,* and *Penthouse* magazines. (Perhaps you are saddened, as I was, to learn these magazine publishers would even include children in them.) Cartoons or photos of children were used six to fourteen times *per issue.* Fifty percent pictured children ages *three to eleven* and all showed the children as participants in, or victims of, sexual activities and/or violence. Most of the children in these pictures appeared unharmed by the abuse, with some pictures even suggesting the children were benefited by it.[11] These three magazines alone (and they certainly are not all the ones on the market) have 27.5 million readers per issue, and 25 percent of these readers are professional men.[12]

We can't really be surprised then when we learn that a woman is raped every six minutes in this country, and that sexual abuse of children is alarmingly epidemic.

Teenage Sexual Behavior
- Three thousand teenage girls become pregnant each day.
- One million teenage girls become pregnant each year, a ratio of one out of every ten.
- Four out of five pregnant teenage girls are unmarried.
- Over 50 percent of teenage pregnancies end in abortion; among the rest who give birth, 30,000 girls are younger than age fifteen.
- In 1991, 20,000 children, ages six to fifteen were diagnosed with AIDS.
- Fifty percent of sexually active males had their first sexual experience between ages eleven and thirteen.
- In a poll of major problems students ages thirteen to twenty face, 99 percent ranked premarital sex as the foremost problem.
- Sixty to seventy-five percent of high school students have some type of sex education class before graduation[13]

Teenagers are sexually active in greater numbers and at younger ages. Their behavior dismays parents, educators, ministers, and society at large. More and more of them are receiving sex education. Their knowledge base about sexuality is the highest of any generation. What prompts this high incidence of sexual behavior among teenagers?

We've already briefly considered the sexual wallop packed in some popular music and other media. One sex educator insisted that the sexually explicit nature of music and of advertising's billion-dollar message so saturates adolescents' lives that their behavior is inevitably altered.[14] If in one year of TV programming there were 20,000 instances of "suggested sexual intercourse,"[15] imagine the cumulative effect of TV through childhood and adolescence.

John Nieder calls this experience "moral abuse," defined as "the violation of a child's innocence which occurs when a child is exposed to sexual information he cannot comprehend or that overwhelms his moral defenses."[16]

Remember your infant child? Not only innocent, but vulnerable? Perhaps there was no clearer symbol of vulnerability than the top of his head where the bones had yet to join. Remember cautioning the inexperienced (or those you simply didn't trust!), "Don't touch his head! Be careful of her head!"

Nieder is suggesting to us that the effect of this moral abuse on our children is as traumatic as an injury to an infant's head. In both cases, the child is attacked at his most vulnerable and indefensible spot and the effects are lifelong.

Some teenagers are seeking to impress peers, or to "keep" a boyfriend or girlfriend through sexual means. Most adults have little patience with such reasons for teenage sex and pregnancy. Some teenagers who feel unsuccessful at school may deliberately become pregnant to avoid feeling unsuccessful. Other pregnant teens receive focused attention for the first time in their lives as the family rallies to deal with the pregnancy.

Our children and teenagers are living in the aftermath of the "sexual revolution," and they've never known differently in their lifetimes. David Elkind believes that our society thrusts a "premature adulthood" on its teenagers and expects them to meet challenges and make decisions with the skill of a middle-aged adult.[17]

Reaping the Sexual Whirlwind

Parenting our preadolescents and young adolescents means losing our fear of their sexual curiosity. Realize that, as their natural curiosity about themselves and their growth increases, they are surrounded by the sexually explicit messages of their society and the sexually active life-styles of teens just older than they. In this day, it is more likely that their sexual curiosity will be manifested in sexual experimentation at an earlier age—during these preadolescent years.

Understanding masturbation is one area where your child needs your direct help, especially your male child. Group pressure to try masturbation may begin in grade school. Boys can hurt themselves physically, like one fifth grader who tried masturbating with his buddies before he had sexually matured. He had a double rupture—his testicles moved back into his body to the pre-birth location. Afraid to talk about it, getting no medical attention, this ten-year-old concluded he was turning into a girl and becoming a homosexual.

And what about A-A? This masturbatory activity which began as a cult practice in the early 1900's is autoerotic asphyxia. To achieve a sexual high, one masturbates while disturbing the flow of blood to the brain through use of a rope, plastic bag, or shoestring. If it kills over 1,000 teenagers a year[18] (and it does), how many more are engaged in this potentially deadly experiment? Twice as many? Ten times?

Preteens and teenagers are susceptible to drawing wrong conclusions about homosexuality. It is another critical sexual topic where your preteen needs your direct help. One study of male homosexual adults asked the participants when they were first aware of their attraction to boys or men. Their responses:

67% — Before age 10
18% — Between 10 and 16
15% — Between 17 and 25[19]

Anecdotal evidence indicates that many practicing adult homosexuals:

- had one or two same-sex encounters as preteens or young teens,
- concluded that they were homosexuals because of these encounters,
- had little or no guidance as they drew that conclusion, and
- so assumed that a homosexual life-style was their actual sexual preference as adults, and acted so.

Preteens and teenagers typically reject homosexuality, what they know of it. That is why it upsets them to think they might be so inclined. That is why the locker room encounters or sex play at sleepovers needs to be interpreted and explained to them.

There are two additional reasons to be informed about homosexuality and be ready to help your preteen with his questions.

1. Parents, just like their children, can misinterpret certain behaviors and draw incorrect conclusions. A boy who never develops an interest in sports, who really likes his male math teacher, may wonder, "Does this mean I'm gay?" His parents may wonder the same thing. But no one can affirm a child's personhood and sexuality like a parent can. Children like this boy need reassurances that liking his teacher and not liking sports do not brand him "homosexual." Parents who stumble onto behaviors, such as mutual masturbation, may fear the worst and say the worst to children. Nothing would propel a child toward continued interest in an occasional homoerotic tendency than for parents to decide he is gay and can't be changed. Likewise, nothing would correct such a child's thinking more than for parents to discourage the behavior and encourage appropriate exploration of sexual questions and curiosity.

Note the importance of understanding masturbation in order to effectively deal with the issue of homosexuality, too.

2. Homosexuality is largely regarded in society as a viable, alternative

life-style. Due to the gay liberation movement of the 70s and the militancy of its leaders, these are a few of the objectives and beliefs of gay-rights advocates:

- Homosexuals should be permitted to be gay any place, any time.
- Government taxes should be used to perform free sex change operations on homosexuals whenever they are demanded.
- Children should be taught in school about all kinds of human sexuality. They should not be told that one mode is healthier, more normal, or better than any other.
- Homosexuals should be given positions as caregivers and permitted to become teachers, clergy, counselors, therapists, and social workers; they should participate in the rearing and education of children.
- All laws against sodomy, homosexuality, pederasty, sado-masochism, and any other form of sexual behavior between consenting adults done in private should be repealed.
- Homosexuality should be taught as a method of birth control and population control.[20]

Masturbation and homosexuality are two subjects you need to be informed about in order to answer your children's questions and guide them based on Christian principles.

Teaching and Telling

- Knowing my child is a delightful, awesome task and one that will continue until he or she is an adult.
- Knowing the world my child is growing up in often is a frustrating, frightening task for which I feel so inadequate.
- Knowing myself as a parent is important, too.

These three foundation blocks support me as I teach my child about sexuality. Some days they seem enough. Many days they wobble and almost topple me into confusion. The only sure foundation in this troubled area, like every significant area of my life and my family's, is the Lord, the Master Designer who knows His plan and loves His people.

The first step we parents take as sex educators, even before we encourage them to read the book for preadolescents, *Sex! What's That?*, is this: Learn what our children already know. What information, what language, what attitudes have they stored away as facts? At this point in time, determine: Is my primary job to add to their knowledge? correct their misinformation? help them internalize Christian values about sexuality? equip them to make good choices? teach them how to protect themselves? Just how far past the stork has your little bird flown? It's time to find out!

What Do I Teach?
1. Study together the Bible's teaching on the role of parents as teachers. A strange place to begin for sex education? Not really. We

parents need to hear and apply the strong scriptural passages about being our children's instructors. Our children need to hear it as an important lesson for living and growing up in a Christian home.

• *Deuteronomy 6:4-9* This beloved passage depicts daily family life, from dawn to dusk, as the best classroom for teaching the Lord's way to our children. Remember, others will teach your child facts about reproduction and birth control. You will probably not like everything they present or the way they give sexual information to your children. We parents are the only ones who can ensure that our children are taught values to shape their decisions and behavior.

• *Proverbs 4:1-11,20-27* This passage echoes the Ten Commandments' promise of long life to the child who honors his parents: "Listen, my son, accept what I say, and the years of your life will be many" (v. 10, NIV).

• *Proverbs 5* This wonderful passage emphasizes the importance of listening to and following instructions. It warns against sexual temptation, describes the suffering or consequences of sexual sin, and exalts the joy of marriage. It may help you more than your child right now because it speaks rather frankly. Your child *is* ready to hear its conclusion: "For a man's ways are in full view of the Lord, and he examines all his paths. The evil deeds of a wicked man ensnare him; the cords of his sin hold him fast" (Prov. 5:21-22, NIV).

• *Ephesians 6:4* This verse speaks for itself: "Fathers, do not exasperate your children; instead, bring them up in the training and instruction of the Lord" (NIV).

2. Know where the Bible speaks about sexuality. Turn to it first when answering your children's questions. As a guide to Bible study, study the section earlier in this book, "Biblical Foundations," by Michael Fink.

John Nieder, in his book *What You Need to Tell Your Child About Sex*, categorizes the following key passages and teachings:[21]

• *Genesis 1:27-28; 2:18-25* God created two distinct sexes. He created marriage for life. The sexual relationship was commanded before sin entered the world.

• *2 Samuel 13:1-20* Wrong friends lead you to wrong behavior. Avoid situations that compromise your values. Sexual sin deceives you and others; it may produce irrational behavior, alienation from others, hatred of others, even violence toward others. Its damage can't be undone.

• *Proverbs 5; 6:20-35; 7* These three chapters are filled with warnings about the dangers of adultery and the need to flee temptation.

• *1 Corinthians 6:9-20* The habitual sexual sinner may not be a Christian. Our bodies are important enough to be resurrected; they belong to God, not to immoral behavior. Flee, don't fight, temptation. Sexual sin can hurt us and our bodies; and it can be forgiven. God confirms His ownership of us by the Holy Spirit within us. Because of Jesus' bodily sacrifice for us, we should honor Him with our bodies.

- *1 Corinthians 7:1-9* Unmarried people have greater freedom to serve. Sex outside of marriage is wrong. The solution for passion is a spouse, not a boyfriend or girlfriend. Husbands and wives have natural sexual desires for each other; they should have access to each other's bodies. A couple's spiritual union and physical union are both important. Freedom in marriage with your spouse reduces sexual temptation.

- *1 Thessalonians 4:1-8* Our purity pleases God; it is His will for us. God wants us to learn to control our bodies and desires in holy, honorable ways. Sex outside of marriage takes advantage of the other person. Disregarding these instructions is rejecting God's instructions.

3. Teach your children that a pure life is God's plan for them. One educator has said, "In today's culture, we have to give kids permission *not* to have sex."[22] For us as Christians, the Bible's clear teaching is that purity is much more than restraint from certain acts. It involves purity in my mind, in the thoughts I have toward another person. Jesus clearly told us, "Anyone who looks at a woman lustfully has already committed adultery with her in his heart" (Matt. 5:28, NIV).

Our "tweens" and teens have an interesting way of thinking. Have you ever heard questions like: "How much do I have to eat before I can be excused from the dinner table?" "How long do I have to play outside before I can watch TV?" Or, a bit tougher: "If I accidentally see someone's test paper, is it really cheating to use his answer?" In other words, our kids frequently want to know: "How much can I get away with before I am in trouble? Where's the outer limit so I'll know how far I can go?"

Do you see the implications of this kind of thinking in making decisions about sexual behavior? The challenge for parents is to present purity as the plumb line for making decisions about sexual attitudes and actions. A Christian view of sexuality does not ask, "How far from purity can I wander before I have sinned?" It guides me to turn toward purity and seek it in my attitudes and actions.

Your "tweenager" or teenager needs to know that stirrings of attraction to the opposite sex are natural. He needs to know the difference between lust and love, especially as the Bible explains this. She needs to know the powerful grip that sexually titillating or explicit materials can have on her mind. Chapter 4 in the book, *Sex! What's That?*, would be good to read and discuss together.

Teach your children this important distinction. In the Bible, we are told to *fight* to live the Christian life, that this is a lifelong fight, but one we can win because of Christ's victory in our lives (see 1 Cor. 9:26; 1 Tim. 6:12; 2 Tim. 4:7). We are also told to *flee* temptation, *not* to fight it (see 1 Cor. 6:18; 1 Tim. 6:11; 2 Tim. 2:22; Jas. 4:7). Staying pure depends on a consistent response to temptation—and that is to get away from it as quickly as possible.

4. Teach your child how to evaluate situations and make decisions. Dan Yeary has suggested that any decision we make is enced by at least these fifteen major influences:[23]

JESUS CHRIST	FRIENDS AND PEERS
LOCAL CULTURE	WORLD POWERS
THE BIBLE	FAMILY
LAWS	PERSONAL HEALTH
THE ENVIRONMENT	THE CHURCH
OTHER AUTHORITIES	COACHES AND TEACHERS
SOCIETY IN GENERAL	EVIL FORCES
HISTORY	

Your child will feel the impact of all these influences but is probably not aware of all of them, nor very interested in them when it's time to make a decision.

How can a ten- to thirteen-year-old effectively sort through all the sexual messages and misinformation in our society and be a good decision maker? Children need a simple tool, something easy to remember. Something like these three tests:

The Test of Secrecy: Would I be embarrassed or ashamed if my family and best friends knew what I was doing or thinking?

The Test of Universality. Would it still seem right if everyone else did the same thing I am doing? What kind of families, churches, and communities would we have if everybody decided to act this way?

The Test of Prayer. Can I pray about it? Can I honestly ask God to bless this decision and anything that will result from this decision?[24]

Interestingly, the famous researcher on death and dying, Elisabeth Kubler-Ross, gives this excellent summary statement: "Make your choices based on love, not fear."[25] Matthew 22:39 says you are to love the Lord and other people.

5. Teach how God expects us to treat other people through studying the "one another" passages. The most famous of all these biblical passages is " . . . we must love one another. This is how we know what love is: Christ gave his life for us. We, too, ought to give our lives for our brothers" (1 John 3:11,16, GNB). Of all the things true of love, this is utterly clear: love is unselfish and other-directed, to its very core. Any action which compromises the health or security of another is not loving; any action which promotes me ahead of another is not loving.

Like "love one another," the rest of the "one another" passages were written to Christian people, instructing them how to treat each other. What are we to do for one another?

- Be devoted to (Rom. 12:10, NIV)
- Honor (Rom. 12:10, NIV)
- Live in harmony with (Rom. 12:16, NIV)
- Stop passing judgment on (Rom 14:13, NIV)
- Be likeminded toward (Rom. 15:5, KJV)
- Accept (Rom. 15:7, NIV)
- Instruct (Rom. 15:14, NIV)
- Care for (1 Cor. 12:25, NASB)

- Serve (Gal. 5:13, NIV)
- Bear burdens of (Gal. 6:2, NASB)
- Bear with (Eph. 4:2, NIV)
- Be kind and compassionate to (Eph. 4:32, NIV)
- Forgiving (Eph. 4:32, KJV)
- Submit to (Eph. 5:21, NIV)
- Comfort (1 Thess. 4:18, NASB)
- Encourage (1 Thess. 5:11, NASB)
- Confess your sins to (Jas. 5:16, NASB)
- Pray for (Jas. 5:16, NASB)

All these unselfish actions describe our Lord. He showed us the possibility of living life, of making decisions, of relating to other people with another's benefit in mind. The ultimate test of love is not how I am loved, but how loving I am to others. It is this kind of love we try to teach our children from the time they are very small. "Share your toys with Bobby." "To have a friend, you must be a friend." Or, the one my own children sometimes despair of, coming one more time from my mouth, "We take the initiative. No matter what someone else does, we act toward them first in a loving way." Why? Because Christ has already gone before us in this way and asks His disciples to follow.

Jesus promises us, His modern disciples, the same as He promised His first disciples, struggling to live His life in a hostile, unsympathetic world: "In this world you will have trouble. But take heart! I have overcome the world" (John 16:33, NIV).

How Do I Teach?

"Train a child in the way he should go, and when he is old he will not turn from it" (Prov. 22:6, NIV).

Probably this is the most concise, oft-quoted verse describing our educative role as parents. It reads like a guarantee, making parenting sound like a win-every-time proposition. We know better than to be so glib with Scripture.

By using several different sources, there is another way to phrase this verse and explore its meaning:

Start[26] a child according to his way, that is, in keeping with his unique personality, temperament, and aptitude[27], and when he is out from under your parental authority[28], he will not turn from it.

Stated so, this verse affirms several truths we've already encountered:

- Know your child in his uniqueness.
- Respond to your child's questions, needs, and growth through understanding how she changes and matures.
- Make your ultimate parenting goal to raise a child who will be an independent, self-disciplined adult.

We've already referred to Deuteronomy 6:4-9. Read it from your

Bible again. Not only do these verses instruct parents to teach their children, but they encourage us to do it creatively! Try rewriting verses 7-9 with updated images. I have asked parents to do this, and they will say:

"Talk to them while driving the carpool, on the way to church, walking around the block."

"Greet your kids with a Scripture thought or praise for the new day as you wake them."

"Put Scriptures or encouragements under the magnets on the refrigerator."

"Wear symbols of your faith on key rings, as necklaces, clipped to backpacks."

You get the idea! Whatever the subject at hand, there's no need to be boring! Use your knowledge of your child's uniqueness in combination with varieties of techniques to impress God's truth and values upon them.

Most of all, as you take on the teaching responsibility for sexuality with your children, remember how many topics it includes. No parent wants to feel he or she must talk only about sexual acts and body parts in order to instruct children about sex. As a thorough sex educator, you and your child will be talking about:

MARRIAGE	STDS AND AIDS	GOD'S PURPOSE
ATTITUDES	FRIENDSHIP	FOR FAMILIES
PARENTING	DECISION MAKING	RESPECT FOR
BEHAVIOR	SELF-ESTEEM	OTHERS
CHILDREN	INDEPENDENCE	SELF-CONTROL
PURITY	ABSTINENCE	
MEDIA	TRUSTWORTHINESS	
TRUST	TEMPTATION AND SIN	

This list is not meant to overwhelm you, but to reassure you that many topics will help your child understand the beauty and purpose of their sexuality.

1. Role-play with them and their siblings. Let children play adult roles while you take the children's roles. If you see a TV show or ad that misrepresents God's view of sexuality, play it again so that His view is upheld.

2. Use any word games you have, like Scrabble or Boggle, to help children learn the vocabulary of sexuality.

3. Discuss songs you hear on the radio or movies their friends want them to see. Apply the three tests of decision making about right and wrong to the behaviors and attitudes depicted in the media.

4. Start a Summer Sexuality Scrapbook. During summer vacation, you and your "tweenager" make this a joint project. Put in print ads that carry sexual messages. Copy in it slogans, bumper stickers, lines from movies or songs. Include Bible verses and drawings of Bible heroes who resisted temptation. Discuss each entry as you make it, or set a time each week to pull out the scrapbook and see what is new in it.

5. Play "What's Wrong with This Picture?" as you see billboards or observe the attitudes or actions of "tweens" or teens.

6. Install a question box at home where anyone can leave a question. Plan to discuss during family meetings or at a set time each week.

7. At annual checkups during these "tweenage" and teenage years, help them formulate questions to ask their doctor about how they are growing and what they can expect.

8. Help them make a gradual transition from only having same-sex friends to including opposite-sex friends.

9. Introduce them to heroes. Too many "tweenagers," who like to look up to somebody, are fixated on sports stars and rock musicians. These heroes may not be the ones to inspire your children to aspire to God's best for their lives.

So, talk about important people you admire. Get books or rent movies about people who made good choices, who respected others. Help them find and admire a biblical hero—Ruth, Priscilla and Aquila, Timothy, Barnabas, Jeremiah, Lydia.

10. Plan special outings just for the purpose of teaching certain things to your child. Go to a favorite fast-food place, on a leisurely walk, fishing, camping, or on an overnight stay. See such special outings as one of *many* talks you and your child will have about important issues, not as *"The Talk"* parents dread and try to do once and for all.

Barry and Carol St. Clair suggest just such a special outing at these critical times:[29]

With your son:
- Before puberty begins—Understanding the male body and how it changes.
- At puberty—Understanding nocturnal emissions and masturbation.

With your daughter:
- Before puberty begins (generally earlier than for a boy)—Understanding the female body and how it changes.
- Before any signs of sexual development—Understanding menstruation and any fears concerning it.

Chapter 2 in the book, *Sex! What's That?*, will be a helpful tool for discussing these topics.

Who Else Is Teaching My Child?

We've looked at the impact of media messages on sexuality. You're aware that peers spread a special brand of misinformation.

I want to caution you to take an active interest in the sex education stance of your children's school. These years, and the adolescent years which follow, will include some type of sex education through their school experience.

We cannot explore it at length here; and it varies so much from one curriculum to another, and from one school to another. However, there are some disturbing general characteristics beginning to emerge:

1. Secretiveness. Some curricula instruct teachers to withhold specific information about the course content from parents. One which did so included explicit color slides of both heterosexual and homosexual intercourse, and audiocassettes of homosexual and lesbian lovers describing their sexual pleasures.[30]

2. Disclaimers about values taught in the course. Some curricula deny that values are taught in their materials. You and I would read through their material and conclude that the value of abstinence, of heterosexual love, of marriage as the time for complete sexual expressions are the only values *not* taught. What values do you think are at the very least implicit in a sex education course that includes films of boys describing how intercourse feels with a virgin? or asks students to sculpt genitalia in modeling clay? or teaches street language for varieties of sexual activities? or has time to practice fitting a condom on cucumbers? or takes field trips to abortion clinics and walks through the admission and treatment procedures? or pictures parents as limited and ineffective, but sex educators as competent and wise?[31]

Some sex education materials teach that a child's values do not have to agree with parents' values. They teach fun, safe ways to have sex. They encourage "virginity with affection," sometimes known as "outercourse" for those not yet ready for sexual activity.

3. Confusion over the result of sex education courses. The myriad surveys which try to evaluate the effectiveness of these courses publish many different results. One thing seems to be clear: that even though sex education leads to increased use of contraceptives, this is offset by the rise of teenage sexual activity.[32]

Be informed by asking these questions of the sex education curriculum chosen for your children at every grade in their school experience:

• Does the program encourage young people to engage in sexual intercourse or does it send a clear message of abstinence and self-restraint?

• Does it violate community standards of taste and decency?

• Does it present traditional viewpoints toward sexuality in comparable detail and with the same degree of objectivity or sympathy as more permissive viewpoints?

• What selection process was used in choosing the program?

• What is its purpose?[33]

• Can parents exercise a right to remove their children from a sex education class of which they do not approve and instruct them with other materials or curricula?

Postscript to Parents

We know that children and adolescents have a special brand of logic as they look out at the world. They *know* about such horrors as AIDS,

STDs, and teenage pregnancy, but they are convinced that it will not happen to them. They believe that because they do not choose to have a deadly disease or a baby at age fourteen they will not experience those events; if they do, their special logic tells them it was an accident for which they are not responsible.

As adults, we are supposed to be experienced in the fine art of planning ahead, of evaluating causes as to their effects, of thinking about our decisions' impact on others as well as ourselves. How is it that we slip back into an earlier, limited mode of thinking when it comes to teaching our children about sexuality? Could it be that we think our silence protects us and our children? Have we concluded that if we do not talk about sexuality, our children will grow to adulthood untainted by any of its darker side? That is childish logic. And in this particular area of parenting our children, we dare not indulge in it.

Notes

[1]George Kaluger and Meriem Fair Kaluger, *Human Development: The Span of Life*. (St. Louis: Times Mirror/Mosby, 1984) 323-328.

[2]Ibid. 328.

[3]David Elkind, *A Sympathetic Understanding of the Child, Birth to Sixteen*. (Boston: Allyn & Bacon, Inc., 1978) 85-86.

[4]Margaret E. Schultz, "Understanding Adolescent Sexuality." (*The Early Adolescent Magazine*, November, 1986, Vol. I, No. 2) 29.

[5]Tipper Gore, *Raising PG Kids in an X-Rated Society*. (Nashville: Parthenon Press, 1987) 82.

[6]Ibid. 85-86.

[7]James Dobson and Gary L. Bauer, *Children at Risk*. (Dallas: Word Publishing, 1990) 65.

[8]Gore 88.

[9]John Nieder, *What to Tell Your Child About Sex*. (Nashville: Thomas Nelson Publishers, 1991) 24.

[10]Dobson and Bauer 213.

[11]"Children in *Playboy*, *Penthouse* and *Hustler*. (*Preventing Sexual Abuse: A Newsletter of the National Family Life Education Network*, Vol. I, No. 2, 1986) 4.

[12]Ibid.

[13]Statistics compiled from "What's Gone Wrong with Teen Sex?" (*People*, April 13, 1987) 111-121; Elizabeth Stark, "Young, Innocent and Pregnant." (*Psychology Today*, October, 1986) 28-35; Barry and Carol St. Clair, *Talking with Your Kids About Dating, Love and Sex*. (San Bernardino, CA: Here's Life Publishers, 1989) 14-15; and "Aids Kids Go to School." (*Children and Teens Today*, June, 1989) 3.

[14]"What's Love Got to Do with It?' Protecting Teens Against 'Sexploitation' in Advertising." (*Children and Teens Today*, March, 1987) 2-3.

[15]"What's Gone Wrong with Teen Sex?" p. 111.

[16]Nieder 42.

[17]David Elkind, *All Grown Up and No Place to Go: Teenagers in Crisis*. (Reading, Massachusetts: Addison-Wesley, 1984) 3-4.

[18]Nieder 168.

[19]David McWhorter and Andrew Mattison, *The Male Couple*. (Englewood Cliffs, New Jersey: Prentice-Hall, Inc., 1984) 268.

[20]Philip Michael Ukleha, "A Theological Critique of the Contemporary

Homosexual Movement." (Th.D. diss., Dallas Theological Seminary, 1982) 42-44; cited in Nieder 170.

[21]Adapted from John Nieder, *What to Tell Your Child About Sex*. (Nashville: Thomas Nelson Publishers, 1991) 210-212.

[22]Kathy Lipscomb Bridge, *Sex Education for the '90s*. (Portland, Maine: J. Winston Walch, Publisher, 1984, 1991) 80.

[23]Dan Yeary, *Make Up Your Mind!* (Nashville, Tennessee: Convention Press, 1990) 31.

[24]T. B. Maston, *Right or Wrong?* used in Yeary 38.

[25]Elisabeth Kubler-Ross, quoted in Bridge 130.

[26]*New International Version Disciple's Study Bible*. (Nashville: Holman Bible Publishers, 1988), note on Proverbs 22:6. 775.

[27]Dixie Ruth Crase and Arthur H. Criscoe, *Parenting by Grace: Discipline and Spiritual Growth Parent's Guide*. (Nashville: Convention Press, 1987) 28.

[28]Dawson McAllister, *Preparing Your Teenager for Sexuality*. (Irving, Texas: Shepherd Ministries, 1988) P-9.

[29]Barry and Carol St. Clair, *Talking with Your Kids About Love, Sex and Dating*. (San Bernardino, California: Here's Life Publishers, 1989) 86-96.

[30]Linus Wright, "Sex Education: How to Respond." (*The World and I*, September, 1989) 506-507.

[31]Jacqueline R. Kasum, "Sex Education: The Hidden Agenda." (*The World and I*, September, 1989) 491, 497-498, 500.

[32]Ibid. 497.

[33]Wright 509-510.

Just for Parents of Adolescents

Ann Cannon

Sing the Lord's Song

**"How can we sing songs of the Lord while in a foreign land?"
(Psa. 137:4, NIV)**

Parents question how they can sing the Lord's song for sexual purity
in today's foreign land inhabited by their teenagers. The news from
that land is not just bad—it's devastating! In 1991, the Children's
Defense Fund reported these daily events:
- 7,742 teenagers become sexually active
- 632 teenagers develop syphilis or gonorrhea
- 2,795 teenage girls become pregnant
- 1,106 teenage girls have an abortion
- 1,295 teenage girls give birth

By the age of fifteen, 27 percent of the girls and 33 percent of the
boys have experienced sexual intercourse. (The good news is that more
than 60 percent of today's teenagers under fifteen have not become
sexually active. Keep that in mind!)

You will find additional facts and figures in the book for adolescents,
Sexuality: God's Gift. Use it and this section to guide your teenager
through this *foreign land*.

No Longer a Child; Not Yet an Adult

What happened to those cherubic children who yesterday hung on
your every word? Today they make you feel like a mental imbecile. It's
adolescence—a time of change and development. Here is a quick
overview of that development.

Physically, a teenager learns to accept and care for that ever-chang-
ing body. Sporadic growth results in embarrassment, fear, confusion,
and disappointment. Big feet, a long nose, curly hair, short legs, long
arms—the things that make each unique—actually create concern for
each teenager.

Emotionally, a teenager turns from depending on the family for emotional support to self-reliance. Along the way peers, sports personali-
ties, rock stars, and significant others become sources of influence. As
they develop emotional independence, teenagers lash out at authority,

equating freedom with rebellion. Their fragile emotions make every-thing a crisis.

Intellectually, a teenager learns how to process and use information. Younger teenagers think concretely. Everything is right or wrong, black or white. They lack polished communication skills. With no way to share their thoughts, they often sulk and brood. As they begin to think more abstractly, they deal in theory and speculation. They can talk for hours about their latest philosophies. This self-centered nature is normal.

Socially, teenagers learn skills needed to get along with both sexes in a social setting. Initially, same-sex friends are most important. Opposite sex friendships develop later. Social skills evolve as a teenag-er gains control of that growing body and feels personal respect. Peer acceptance strengthens the way a teenager feels about himself or her-self.

Spiritually, a teenager must develop a personal faith. Along the way doubt, confusion, and questions occur. Spiritual growth depends great-ly on other areas of development. A spiritually deep teenager is also emotionally settled, physically secure, and mentally advanced.

Sexually, teenagers must learn to use their new sexuality in a responsible way. Raging hormones keep parents and teenagers on an emotional roller coaster. Hormones can cause illogical behavior, inap-propriate actions, and useless worries making good decisions more dif-ficult.

You have a difficult task in guiding your teenager through these teen years. It takes patience, time, effort, and much prayer. Let this materi-al ease your task as you deal with sexual development.

"When I Was Your Age . . ."

Parents, the five words in the preceding heading are guaranteed to turn off your teenager. Although physical changes remain the same, society has changed the rules on sex. Your teenager faces new pres-sures.

Get in touch with these pressures and struggles by remembering. Also, before talking with your teenager about sex, analyze your *own* fears and attitudes. How would you complete these sentences?

- I feel that sex is . . .
- As a teenager, I thought sex was . . .
- I believe I can help my teenager deal with today's sexual pres-sures by . . .
- The fear I have for my teenager is . . .

What about teenagers' attitudes towards sex? What are their wor-ries? While teenagers fear AIDS and sexually transmitted diseases, studies show that pressures to have sexual intercourse come at a younger age. In fact, one poll taken of the Boys and Girls Clubs of America found that 42 percent felt pressured to have sex. Cutting class was the only thing that caused more pressure (47 percent). By the time they finish high school, seven out of ten teenagers see nothing wrong with sex before marriage.

On the other side, when asked what they most wanted, younger teenagers desired support and love from their families. Even though they don't always show this desire, your unconditional love to that teenager makes a difference. You may not like what he does, but you still can love that one who is your child. Remember God has loved you at times when you were unlovely. Psalm 136 affirms God's unconditional love in many circumstances. Can you share this unconditional love with your teenager?

The Sex Talk

From one thousand teenagers, Josh McDowell discovered that one-third of the girls and 14 percent of the guys had received sexual information from their parents. Most teenagers gain sexual facts from their friends, movies, TV, and magazines. Much is misinformation such as *you can't get pregnant standing up,* fantasy such as *he'll love me if I do it,* and myths such as *everybody's doing it!*

Unfortunately, our parents didn't talk to us about sex, because it was a forbidden topic. This book and *Sexuality: God's Gift* are designed to help you break that pattern of silence.

Many schools offer sex education courses to cover basic physical development. This book and every book in this series goes further. Sexual purity is encouraged, not only for physical reasons, but also for moral, ethical, and religious reasons. Read *Sexuality: God's Gift.* Then encourage your teenagers to read and work through the exercises in it. Spend time together using the book as a focal point for discussion.

Making The Sex Talk Work—Session One

Let these ideas help you share information in a comfortable manner with your teenager.

1. *Encounter.*—Make an appointment with your teenager. Set aside at least thirty minutes. Select a time when neither of you is tired or stressed.

Prior to the appointed time, ask God for wisdom. Pray for an open mind for you and your teenager.

2. *Encourage.*—Begin by thanking your teenager for taking this time to share. State your desire to listen, as well as to talk. If the teenager is already familiar with *Sexuality: God's Gift,* that will help.

3. *Examine.*—Review the crossword puzzle under "Understanding the Sexual Me" in Chapter 1 of *Sexuality: God's Gift.* Be sure your teenager knows these terms. Use the correct words, not slang. Ask: What part of your own sexual growth or that of the opposite sex still confuses you? How do you feel about what is happening to your body?

As you continue in Chapter 1, look over the statements in "I Wish Someone Would Tell Me." Ask: Which of these concern you? Review the terms in "The Right Word." Ask: What terms confuse you?

In Chapter 2, point out how God created sex and sexuality and called both good. Use a Bible to do the matching exercises in "Who Am I Sexually?" and "The Sex Part of Sexuality." Encourage your teenager to mark these verses in their Bible.

Share a time when you realized how commitment in marriage went beyond physical attraction.

Complete the sentences in "When I Was Your Age . . ." in this section of this book. Notice the differences, but don't dwell on the negatives. Share a humorous time when you first started dating.

If your teen is dating, affirm something good you have noticed about that dating. If your teen is not yet dating, affirm the positive qualities that you see in your teenager.

Review the healthy and unhealthy reasons for dating in "The Dating Game" in Chapter 2. Ask: Why are some ideas unhealthy? What might be the results of dating for this reason?

4. *Evaluate.*—Look over the dating contract in "The Dating Game" in Chapter 2. Ask your teenager to fill it out privately, and return later to talk about it. Be prepared to compromise, if necessary.

5. *Embrace.*—Before you finish, set a time for a second session. Hug your teenager and compliment something you see happening in his life.

The Fish Bowl Syndrome

But you followed my teaching, conduct, purpose, faith, patience, love, perseverance (2 Tim. 3:10)

You are the first, and usually, the most influential role model your child has. Your child will either adopt or reject your life-style and values. Of course, younger teenagers tend to rebel against their parents. To them rebellion asserts their independence. However, because the values you taught them as children are deeply ingrained, most return to these as young adults.

Your attitude and actions about sexual matters affect your teenager. How you relate to the opposite sex establishes how your teenager will relate. Your teenager watches your actions towards marriage. If you uphold commitment, faithfulness, love, and support as the basis for marriage, then you model the best marriage can be.

Do not assume that you can say one thing, such as no sex outside of marriage, and act differently. Theory does not impress teenagers so much as actions. If you are a divorced, single parent, hold up the ideals of sexual expression in marriage. Help your teenager understand why your marriage did not work out. If you have remarried, share how compromise and commitment make a new marriage work.

Your values influence your teenager. To determine what you value, look at your checkbook and your calendar. Your values are based on where you spend your money, time, and effort. You indicate the value of your teenager by taking time to offer guidance during these growing up years.

The Key to Keeping Kids

The key is communication that begins early. If your teenager felt comfortable as a child talking to you, then that adolescent will probably continue the process. Teenagers talk to parents when parents:

* do not judge. Remember, some teenagers take different points of view to test your reaction.
* listen. James 1:19 stresses the importance of listening. That is why God gave us two ears and only one mouth.
* appear interested. Do not *tell* when you can *talk*. Telling is the authority voice that says to do it this way, or else. Talking is a two-way conversation where each person's input is respected.

In talking with your teenager about sex, provide complete and accurate information. Use the correct terms. The words in chapter 1 and "The Right Word" in all chapters of *Sexuality: God's Gift* do that.

In your talks, don't assume anything. Teenagers assume that parents will think *they're doing it!* if they ask questions. Adults assume teenagers know all the answers. Avoid false assumptions. Be open to all ideas.

While it is important to be honest with teenagers, they are not marriage counselors. It is inappropriate to discuss specific sexual activities or marital problems with your teenager. If you are a single parent, it is also inappropriate to discuss dates, except in a general manner.

As you talk about sex with your teenager, set boundaries, not barriers. Barriers list *do's* and *don'ts* that create rebellion. Placing blame, excessive discipline, and unidentified rules build barriers, not boundaries. Compromise and cooperation create boundaries. Try to balance your limitations with acceptance and trust. Boundaries work effectively when teenagers and parents sit down and set limits together.

Making the Sex Talk Work—Session Two

Use these procedures to help you plan your discussion with your teenager. You may choose other, less structured, approaches, too. TV shows, for example, may provide contexts for discussion. Use these teachable moments wisely.

1. *Establish.*—Set an appointed time like you did before. Sunday afternoons might be a good time. Pray for the time you spend with your teenager.

2. *Encourage.*—Affirm the positive experience you had last time. Ask: Is there anything that we discussed last time that you still want to talk about? What helped you the most?

Remind your teenager that you will not judge his or her ideas or questions. Encourage your teenager to be open and frank.

3. *Examine.*—Ask: Why do some teenagers have sex before marriage? Why do others say *no* to sex before marriage? Compare your teen's

responses to the graffiti boxes in "Just Say No and Mean It" in Chapter 3 of *Sexuality: God's Gift*.

Read the case study about Lanie and Ted in "Operate with Caution" in Chapter 4. Let your teenager make the choices. Look at the other choices. Ask: How do teenagers get into positions where sex *just happens?*

Acknowledge that many teenagers try sexual intercourse to rebel against their parents. Many others seemed surprised by the strong emotions they feel, even after making a commitment to sexual purity. Encourage your teenager not to be shocked by strong sexual desire. Share a time when you faced sexual temptation and how you handled it.

Examine reasons to remain pure. Review the sexually transmitted diseases under "Truth and Consequences" in Chapter 3 as you fill in the chart. Identify facts about AIDS, pregnancy, and abortion. Your teenager may already have an opinion on abortion. This is often a hot topic in current event classes, as well as in sex education. Look at the verses under "The Truth About Abortion" in Chapter 3 as you discuss the value of human life.

Point out how the fantasy of premarital sex leading to a successful marriage is portrayed in media. It is not always that way in real life. Evaluate one or two of the situations in "Happily Ever After" in Chapter 3. Ask: Why did sex before marriage cause problems in these marriages? Which problem surprised you? Why?

Ask: Do you know what safe sex is? Point out that sex outside of marriage is sin. Note that from God's point of view sin is never safe. Explain that safe sex is an unnecessary term if a person says *no* to sex before marriage.

To summarize the reasons for saying *no* to sex before marriage, see who will be first to unscramble the words in "Why Stay Pure?" in Chapter 4. Share your personal reasons for remaining pure.

4. *Evaluate.*—Review the three tests for deciding if an action is right or wrong by looking in "Just Say *No* and Mean It" in Chapter 3. Encourage your teenager to mark these verses in their Bible.

Summarize by asking your teenager to complete the sentences in "All You Ever Wanted to Know About Sex, But Were Afraid to Ask" in Chapter 4.

5. *Enable.*—Explain that the Bible does not deal with all issues of sexuality. Point out, however, that the truths of the Bible apply to all areas of life. Point out the truths in "Sex in the Bible" in Chapter 4. Match these truths with the Bible passages. You might want to discuss how one or two of the truths apply to sexual purity.

Ask: Based on what we have talked about, how do you feel about sexual purity? Have you made any decision about how you will handle sexual pressures? What are your main reasons?

Do not push your teenager to agree with your point of view. A commitment will be much more effective, and lasting, if your teenager takes that step himself.

If your teenager decides to remain pure, sign the commitment card in "All You Ever Wanted to Know About Sex, But Were Afraid to Ask" in Chapter 4.

After talking with his son and his daughter about sexual purity, one doctor/father gave each a ring to symbolize that pledge of purity. You might consider a similar gesture.

Pray together about this commitment.

Look for additional opportunities to talk about sexual purity as your teenager continues to develop. One mother uses current events as the basis for her discussions. She watches for popular movies, the most popular songs, or related news stories. Then she brings up the topic at the dinner table. Everyone discusses the topic, and her teenager gets to hear a Christian's point of view.

Addressing the Issue of Birth Control

There are some issues not covered in *Sexuality: God's Gift* that may or may not surface in discussions with your teenager. Nevertheless, you need to be prepared to confront these tough issues. You will need to determine the appropriate time.

For example, you may choose to wait until late adolescence or right before marriage to discuss birth control with your son or daughter. What follows provides a way to assist you in that discussion. Be aware that your discussion of this material may communicate acceptance and approval of non-Christian behavior prior to marriage. Make sure you clearly affirm the biblical teachings of abstinence before marriage. Place the discussion of birth control in the context of information that should only be implemented after marriage. The following chart was prepared by Karen Dockrey using the following sources: "Birth Control," *U.S. News and World Report*, December 24, 1990; *American Medical Association Home Medical Encyclopedia*, 1989.

Don't Lose That Loving Feeling

In the process of talking with your teenager, you may discover that he has already become involved in sexual activity. Perhaps your teenager has been sexually abused without your knowledge. Maybe a son has had a homosexual encounter and is extremely embarrassed and confused. Or perhaps curiosity, peer pressure, or poor information has caused your teenager to experiment with different degrees of sex.

This will be difficult for you, but you are not without hope. God has an infinite capacity to forgive; you can, too. Many young people who were previously sexually active have taken a vow of sexual purity. This desire for second virginity is very effective.

Pray with your teenager for forgiveness. Then forgive your child. Remember, we are all children whom God has forgiven.

Those who sow in tears shall reap with joyful shouting (Ps. 126:5, NAS). This verse brought hope to me during my children's teen years. One day you, too, will reap that joyful shouting.

METHOD	EFFECTIVE-NESS*	DISCUSSION
Diaphragm A dome of thin rubber with a coiled metal spring enclosed in the rim. After covering it with spermicide, a woman inserts the diaphragm like a tampon. It opens to cover the cervix. The diaphragm works by keeping the sperm from reaching the ovum (egg). A diaphragm must be fitted by a doctor but after initial purchase, the only cost is spermicide which is available in drugstores.	84%	This method is virtually risk free with effectiveness approaching that of the pill. It can be inserted as early as six hours before intercourse and interferes in no way with sexual pleasure. Its one disadvantage is that the couple must be committed to using it each time. The diaphragm and condom are called barrier methods because they put a barrier between the sperm and ovum.
The Pill This oral contraceptive consists of synthetic progesterone and sometimes estrogens. It works by keeping ovulation from occurring. A doctor must write a prescription and be seen annually for a checkup.	94-97%	This contraceptive is controversial. Some focus on its effectiveness and ease of use; others on its dangerous side effects that include short or long-term infertility after stopping use, headaches, nausea, dizziness, weight gain or loss, breast tenderness, and mood changes. The pill may contribute to heart disease and some types of cancer. It may prevent other types of cancer. The negative effects occur because the pill interferes with the normal hormonal cycle of the woman.

*The percentage of couples using this method who avoid pregnancy in a year. Studies vary, so a range is given.

METHOD	EFFECTIVENESS	DISCUSSION
Condom This easy to obtain contraceptive works by catching the sperm at the end of the penis and not allowing it to enter the vagina or cervix. It works by keeping the sperm from reaching the ovum (egg). No doctor visit is necessary. Condoms are available at drugstores.	86%	This method became popular when publicity credited it with reducing the spread of AIDS and sexually transmitted diseases. Of course the best protection against these is monogamous sex (one partner for life). Advantages of condoms include their easy availability and lack of side effects. Disadvantages include reducing the man's and sometimes the woman's sexual pleasure, the need to put it on when the penis is erect, and ineffectiveness of condoms when they break.
Rhythm Also called the symptothermal method, this method works by observing signs of ovulation and avoiding sexual intercourse during those times. Just before ovulation, a woman experiences a watery discharge or mucous from her vagina. This indicates that she can become pregnant. Her temperature also rises slightly. This method works by not having sex during fertile times.	80%	Couples who choose rhythm have no side effects, pills, or apparatus to bother with. They need a strong motivation to abstain from sexual intercourse during fertile periods and find other expressions of love. This method fails when a couple has sex right before a fertile period and conceives or when a woman misinterprets her fertility. This is the most natural form of contraception for those who don't mind a potential pregnancy.

Norplant This no fuss method works by surgically implanting six progesterone-laden capsules inside the upper arm. Each capsule is about the size of a match stick. They trickle progesterone into the woman's bloodstream which signals the pituitary glands to stop releasing the two hormones necessary for ovulation. Works by stopping ovulation.

99%

This method is new and though extensively tested does not have a long enough track record to know its risks and side effects. Because it interferes with the body's normal hormonal processes, it may create problems. In tested women, fertility returns the next menstrual cycle after the implants are removed. Requires minor surgery. Very expensive.

Cervical Cap A latex rubber device that fits tightly over the cervix and is inserted by the woman. A doctor must fit the woman. A barrier method that works by keeping sperm and the ovum apart.

73-92%

Good for couples who like the low risk of barrier methods but cannot use the diaphragm or don't like the reduced pleasure of the condom.

Sponge This disposable circular foam sponge is about two inches in diameter and two inches thick. It works by killing sperm and keeping surviving sperm and the ovum apart.

72-82%

This contraceptive is easily available but not as effective as other methods.

Spermicides These sperm killers come in various forms including foams, creams, jellies, and tablets. It works by killing sperm.

79%

Spermicides are messy and must be inserted close to the time of intercourse. It may interfere with spontaneity. It is also not as effective as other methods. It can be purchased in drug stores but only with a prescription.

METHOD	EFFECTIVE-NESS	DISCUSSION
Sterilization For men, sterilization is called having a vasectomy and is a simple outpatient procedure. Female sterilization is called a tubal ligation and is major surgery. In men the vas deferens are cut and tied. In women the fallopian tubes are cut and tied, constricted, clipped, or cauterized.	99%	This permanent birth control method is chosen by couples who have had all the children they plan to have. It can be reversed but is expensive and not guaranteed. It is best when a couple definitely decides to have no more children.
Hope Also called, "I didn't mean to get pregnant." This birth control method is not birth control at all.	0%	To avoid pregnancy, you must practice abstinence or use one of the previously described birth control methods. If you are unmarried, practice abstinence. If you are married and do not want a child, use one of the methods previously described. Sexual intercourse without birth control means you are willing to take responsibility for the life you may create.

Church Leaders Supporting Parents

Training Parents in Providing Christian Sex Education

Carolyn Jenkins

Preparing the Church

Sexuality is a sensitive subject for many adults. Perhaps talking about this subject at church is new to your congregation. If so, pave the way ahead of time. Read carefully "Parents and Church Leaders Working Together" in the first part of this book before you continue reading this section. That chapter recommends an initial orientation meeting with parents to assess interest. The material in this section is for training parents in churches that have decided to conduct Christian Sex Education.

Preparing the Leader

Sexuality is a topic that makes some people uneasy. As the leader, you have the responsibility of setting the tone for the session so that parents can be comfortable. If the session models an ease in discussing sexual matters, parents will better be able to discuss at ease with their children.

If the adults do not know each other or if there are visitors, name tags would be good.

This teaching plan consists of a two-hour span of study with a ten-minute break. The first session is more general in nature; the second hour focuses on specific age groups.

Preparing for the Session

Before the session, prepare the following:
• Gather markers, tape, and paper for name tags.
• Collect several recent newspapers. Circle with a red marker any articles that deal with the misuse of sex. Display these around the meeting room.
• Get three-by-five inch cards or similar paper for Activity 2 in Session 1. Have large sheets of newsprint and markers to record answers.

• Make a poster of Proverbs 22:6, divided into three parts as shown below.

Train up a child	in the way he should go	and when he is old he will not depart from it.
PURPOSE	SCOPE	PRINCIPLE

• Make a handout sheet of the following five purpose statements of this curriculum to help parents.

This material will assist and support parents to:
1. Rear mature, responsible, Christian children who apply biblical principles of sexuality in their everyday living.
2. Educate their children about sexuality and how God intends for it to be expressed.
3. Promote abstinence, chastity, healthy self-esteem, and self-discipline among unmarried children and teenagers.
4. Lead children and teenagers to understand the good that God intended for sexual intercourse within marriage and to encourage them to enjoy that relationship only within a God-ordained covenant marriage.
5. Teach appreciation for the human body as God created, and the responsibility each person has to maintain appropriate boundaries with others.

• Prepare the following statements on note cards, one statement per card. Choose people, one for each card, to read the statements at the beginning of Session 2. Be sensitive as to who you choose and the appropriateness of this activity for your group.

What do you say when your two-year-old son is playing with himself in the grocery cart while you are shopping?

What do you say when your five-year-old has an opposite-sex friend over and you find them partially unclothed?

What do you say when your ten-year-old daughter says, "Mom, a boy at school tried to touch me under my clothes?"

What do you say when your thirteen-year-old wants to go to a movie known for open sexual situations?

What do you say when your sixteen-year-old son comes in from a date with a passion mark/love bite on his neck?

• Provide at least two sheets of large paper, newsprint, tear sheets, etc. for each age group (young children; middle-aged children; preadolescents; and adolescents). Have several markers and tape for each group.

• Have on hand copies of this book and copies of the appropriate age group books, enough for those who will be attending. You will need to decide if the church or each participant will purchase these. You may include the price of the book in a preregistration fee and have participants commit to the training session ahead of time.

- Pray for the sessions and those who will be attending.

Conducting the Session

Session 1 (60 minutes)

1. (5 minutes) Welcome participants as they enter. If applicable, help them get a name tag. Encourage them to walk around the room and look at the newspaper and magazine articles highlighted.

When all have arrived, make introductions, pray, and explain the schedule for the evening (session-break-session). Comment on the articles posted around the room and the misuses of sex prevalent in our society. Lead in a prayer committing the time together to God.

2. (15 minutes) Give out three-by-five inch cards or similar size paper. Ask each parent to write their answer to the following questions on the card you gave them:

- How did you first find out about sexual intercourse?
- How old were you?
- How did you gain additional information?

After most have finished writing, tape large sheets of paper to the wall. Call on willing parents to share their answers to the first two questions. Ask for a recorder to list the ways as parents call them out. Ask another adult to write down ages given. After all who are willing have shared, ask for answers to the third question that haven't already been given. The list may include peers, parents, movies, magazines, TV shows, health classes, sex education classes, sex manuals, novels, mates, etc.

After the listing is complete, ask parents, Which of these ways do you want your child to learn more about his or her sexuality?

Make the point that today's child is bombarded with sexual references in music, television, movies, literature, and advertising. Their knowledge of sex and their attitudes about sex are being influenced daily. Is this the knowledge or the attitudes that we as Christian parents were taught or want taught?

3. (10 minutes) Display the first section of the Proverbs 22:6 passage. Talk briefly about the *purpose* of training as explained in the section, "Biblical Foundations," of this book.

Add the second portion of the verse and explain the *scope* of training.

On adding the third portion, talk about the *principle* stated in the verse and how we can interpret the principle.

4. (10 minutes) Read Genesis 1:26-31. Note that God created us male

and female, spiritual beings like God whom God gave a sexual identity, and declared it "very good." Explain that Scripture gives several purposes for sexual intercourse. Assign the following Bible passages to willing readers. As passages are read, ask the group to identify the purpose declared in each.

Genesis 1:28 (Procreation)
Matthew 19:4-6 (Bonding as one flesh)
Proverbs 5:15-23 and 1 Corinthians 7:3-5 (Pleasure)

State that God created sexual intercourse and also drew boundaries around it so that men and women could have the pleasure, bonding, and procreation in an emotionally healthy environment.

Ask parents to silently read Exodus 20:14, Matthew 15:19-20, and 1 Corinthians 6:12-20. Ask them to make a list of the boundaries they see identified.

Review these points:

- We are created as spiritual beings by God.
- There are boundaries set by God related to our sexuality.

5. (10 minutes) Explain that with these statements in mind, we should consider the purpose of what we teach in sex education. Hand out the list of purpose statements. Ask adults to review each statement and determine if each one is what they want for their children. After they have read the statements, let them share why or why not. Explain that these purpose statements are the foundation upon which this curriculum was prepared.

6. (10 minutes) Instruct participants to turn to the section "Parents and Church Leaders Providing Christian Sex Education." Ask them to underline the hindrances to sex education mentioned in the first five paragraphs as you comment on them:

- Invasion of privacy (ours and theirs)
- Embarrassment
- Feelings from the past and/or present
- No role model
- Don't want to encourage experimentation

Explain that after we take a 10-minute break we will try to examine some of these hindrances as we learn how to provide appropriate sex education for our children, no matter what age they may be.

Break (10 minutes)
You may choose to provide light refreshments for participants. Keep the break period to 10 minutes so as not to loose continuity between sessions.

Session 2 (40 minutes)

1. (3 minutes) As the group regathers, have those chosen stand and read their "What do you say when . . ." cards. Do not ask for answers. Simply let the cards be read in a comfortable way, pausing briefly between the reading of each situation. Say: Each of us faces or has faced these, or similar situations. In this session we will seek ways to respond to our children's questions and experiences.

2. (5 minutes) Ask adults to turn to the section of this material "Parents and Church Leaders Providing Christian Sex Education." Highlight the six essentials to sex education:

- Begin with prayer.
- Have a sure foundation of biblical teaching on sexuality.
- Have good information about anatomy and sexual development.
- Know the child.
- Be a good listener.
- Be a good role model.

3. (17 minutes) Divide the participants into groups of same age children. If they have children in more than one age group, encourage them to decide on one group or, if two parents are present from the same home, each can choose a different age group. The groups might include each of the following or any combination, depending on those present.

Young Children	(ages 4-7 years)
Middle-Aged Children	(ages 8-9 years)
Preadolescents	(ages 10-12 years)
Adolescents	(ages 13-17 years)

Instruct each group to do the following activities and bring back a three-minute report to the whole group. Groups will have five minutes to prepare. If your groups are fairly large, assignments within each group can be divided, allowing a few parents to work on each of the assignments.

a. On one of the large sheets of paper provided, list the developmental characteristics of your age child. (See section of this book, "Understanding Your Child's Development.")

b. Be ready to show and tell to the whole group during a reporting time.

Call time and ask for brief reports. Do not allow one group to dominate; allow time for all to report briefly.

4. (15 minutes) Bring out the previous poster on primary and secondary ways a person learns about sex (Activity 2 in Session 1). Ask parents to note which of those ways is affecting their child at his or her stage of life.

Remind parents of the responsibility inherent in Proverbs 22:6. Distribute the appropriate book(s) to each parent.

Young Children: *Boys and Girls—Alike and Different*
Middle-Aged Children: *My Body and Me*
Preadolescents: *Sex! What's That?*
Adolescents: *Sexuality: God's Gift*

Ask parents to identify the purpose of the resource and how they can use it with their child(ren). Lead the group in identifying the characteristics of the resource. Ask group members to make suggestions and discuss ways they will use the resource(s) with their child(ren).

Also, have them turn to the appropriate section in this book that matches their child. This is in the "Just for Parents of . . ." sections. Ask them to review that section and identify characteristics of that section.

Challenge them to wisely use the appropriate book at home with their child(ren). Pledge your support and further guidance, if needed.

If your church is offering the additional group sessions for preadolescents and adolescents, share information about those. Remind parents that these additional sessions are to support them, but are not designed to take the place of the training they do in the home. Explain that preadolescents and adolescents can participate in the supplementary church sessions only after receiving written approval from their parents. Tell the parents of adolescents that there will be one session they will be invited to attend with their youth. Encourage them to be present.

Also ask parents if it would be beneficial for them to meet again to support one another in providing sex education in the home. Meetings could include just those interested. These parent support group meetings should be informal times with an unstructured agenda. Basic questions to consider at each meeting would be, "How is it going with your child?" and "What issues are you struggling with?" and "What can we join you in celebrating?" Give parents time to make any preparation needed for a future parent support group meeting.

Close with a time of prayer and commitment to training children.

Supplementary Group Study

Even though this Christian Sex Education series is designed for use by parents in the home with their children, some churches may choose to offer a group approach to supplement what parents are doing in the home. The group approach works best with preadolescents and adolescents.

The following supplementary plans are recommended for group study. Each session should be scheduled at a time convenient to parents and their children and fit into the flow of the church program. Length of time for each activity and the number of sessions may vary depending on group size and composition; one- to one-and-a-half hour sessions should provide adequate time for each session.

Plans for supplementary group studies can be initiated by the family enrichment committee, a church staff member, or an interested parent or group of parents. Proper church procedures should be followed to plan and conduct the supplementary studies. (See the section in this book, "Parents and Church Leaders Providing Christian Sex Education," for details.)

Before the Study Begins
1. Carefully choose the leaders. They need to be special people. Consider asking a husband-wife team to be coleaders. Look for a couple that models a healthy, happy, Christian marriage; that has experience teaching the age group; and that will *not* have a child in the group.
2. Provide the leader couple with the resource needed for the children or youth and their parents. Encourage them to prepare for leading this study by:
   • reading this resource and the age-graded resource;
   • checking other sources as needed; and,
   • studying session outlines for the age group they will be leading.
3. In addition to publicity for the children and youth, notify parents with a personal letter. Explain the nature of the sessions and the resources recommended for their children or youth. Secure written parental approval for each child to participate in the group. Urge parents to use the appropriate book with their children or youth at home.
4. Include parents of the children or youth in planning for the study. Discuss with parents ways to help the children feel more at ease during the study. Let them know about any at-home activities suggested which leaders plan to use. Encourage parents to cooperate with these

at-home activities and be supportive of their child's involvement in the group. Ask them to see that their children or youth bring Bibles and books to the sessions.

General Suggestions to Coleaders

1. Inject each session with good-natured humor to ease tensions and embarrassments. Children and youth may feel tense and embarrassed, and most will attempt to cover these with jokes, snickering, or teasing each other. You will gain control in this situation more quickly by laughing a bit and teasing a bit with them, rather than by forbidding the jokes or laughter.

2. Be aware that coed groupings may not be as effective with your group as dividing into two groups—one for boys and one for girls. This is especially true in those sessions that deal with anatomy. There is strength, a level of comfort, and an openness when a man discusses certain topics with boys and a woman talks with girls. There are also subjects that need to be addressed in a coed grouping. Leaders will need to discern which will work best for their group.

3. Consider providing a discreet way for children and youth to ask questions they are uncomfortable voicing in the group. Other suggestions are provided in some of the following material. Here are some examples:

- Hang a Question (instead of Christmas) Stocking in a corner or by the coat rack and encourage them to drop their questions in the stocking. This can be done a couple of weeks before the study begins. It is a good way to promote the study as well as provide a way to ask questions and avoid embarrassment.

- Give the group permission to leave questions on your answering machine.

- Pass out cards during each session. Have everyone write something on the card and hand them to you. Anyone writing a question does not need to sign their name. Assure them that those who ask specific questions will remain anonymous.

4. Parents working with their children and youth at home can deal more directly with body parts and the mechanics of sexual intercourse. The church groups will major more on a biblical and Christian understanding of sexuality. However, at times questions will be asked that may call for body parts to be named in church groups. Leaders must use their discretion about what is appropriate and in good taste. In so far as you decide it is appropriate to name body parts, use correct names. Gently insist that children and youth do the same.

5. Pray as you prepare and as you lead the sessions. Pray for each child and youth attending and his family. Pray for courage, humor, and honesty as you teach about sexuality. Include prayer in each session.

6. Send a card or letter to each prospect for the group. Ask them to come to the first session ready to learn.

Supplementary Group Study for Preadolescents and Young Adolescents

Susan Lanford

This section is designed to equip church leaders to guide preadolescents and young adolescents:

• To understand that God created each of them the same way, but they are all different from each other.
• To identify where they are developmentally, caught between being a child and being a teenager, as well as being male or female.
• To realize that their sexual attitudes are formed by what they allow their eyes to see and their ears to hear unless they deliberately choose to have the same attitude God does.
• To stay on the course of God's best plan for their lives.

Although recommended for four sessions, one session per week, the plans can be conducted over a period of six to eight weeks depending on the depth of discussion and the needs within the group.

Session 1
Made to Be Me

Before the Session
1. Have bright construction paper cut in four-by-six-inch rectangles, markers, a hole punch, and bright strands of yarn for name tags.
2. Set up several interest stations where children can discover answers to questions about the world. For example, put a globe on a table with questions like: How many states touch the Mississippi River? How many countries are on the African continent? How many cities are in Iceland? At other places, put the current *World Almanac*, a dictionary, a Bible atlas, and put several "How many?" questions which each resource answers. Finally, put a book which gives the meaning of first names. Children can look up their names and write the meanings on the backs of their name tags.
3. Make three Scripture cards: Psalm 139:13-16; Genesis 1:26-28 and

2:21-24; Psalm 139:1-6,23-24. Make three title cards: Made to Be You; Made to Be Two; Known Through and Through.

4. Make At-Home Activity cards for each person which say:

- Bring your favorite childhood possession or toy to the next session.
- Before the next session, ask your mom or dad, "How did you know you were changing from a child into a teenager? What was the best part about that change? What was the worst?" Write their answers on the back of this card and bring it to the next session.

5. Write a letter to the parents of each child expressing your joy that you will be working with them to help their children understand God's plan for sexuality. Invite and encourage parental participation. In preparation for the first session, ask parents to tell their child how he or she got his or her name or something special about his or her name.

6. Read "My Body—What It Means to Be Me" in *Sex! What's That?*

During the Session

1. As children enter the room, have them make a name tag. Use the hole punch and yarn to hang name tags around their necks.

2. Send them to the interest stations you've set up in the room. Allow the group to explore several stations while everyone arrives. Mingle with the children and encourage them.

3. Gather the group in one circle. Express your excitement that these boys and girls are going to take part in this special study. Give a brief overview of the four sessions. Be sure to tell about At-Home Activities, and the process you've chosen for getting their questions.

4. Ask for answers to some of the interest station questions. Encourage the group to share what was most interesting to them as they answered the questions. Tie this together with an example using the Mississippi River. Say, **Each state along the Mississippi River is unique (the land, the attitudes of the people, cultures, history, etc.). Yet, there are commonalities (each is a state, each is on the river, etc.). And, there is one main commonality—all are part of the United States.**

5. Say, **We have a lot in common—this world, God's love for us, a church that cares for us. Let's thank Him for all these good things.** Lead the group in prayer.

6. Say, **Our world is so amazing and complex. It shows God's handiwork and design everywhere. But the most amazing and complex part of His creation is YOU. Just think, all of us were conceived and born in the same way, but all of us are different from each other! AMAZING!**

7. Pair everyone with a partner. Have each partner tell the story of how his name was chosen or something special about their name. Then, have each pair join another pair. Ask each partner to briefly introduce his original partner to the new pair by telling his or her

name story. When all four in each group have made their introductions, have the group reassemble in one circle. Ask for two or three great stories to be retold.

8. Hand out the three Scripture cards and three title cards in the group. Have one passage read and ask the title card holders which one is the best title for this passage. Have him stand by the Scripture reader. Repeat the process for the remaining passages and titles. Let the group discuss whether they agree with the pairings. Lead the group to discuss the three Scriptures and their titles, using information from "My Body—What It Means to Me" from *Sex! What's That?* Post the six cards and keep them up during all the sessions. Dismiss with prayer.

Session 2
Is This Really Me?

Before the Session
1. Bring an inflatable ball or bean bag.
2. Prepare five placards: Child, Teenager, Tweenager, Preteen, Preadolescent. Mount each on a stick or ruler.
3. Secure two large sheets of newsprint. Make two strips each of "Timed to Grow" and "Feeling High, Feeling Low."
4. Get old magazines, scissors, and paste for two groups.
5. Read "Preadolescent—and Proud of It," "My Growing—Understanding God's Timing," and " My Feelings—Where Did They Come From?" in *Sex! What's That?*

During the Session
1. Hand out name tags as each child enters. Welcome them back to the group. Ask them to put their name tags on the childhood possession or toy they brought and put it in a special area you have designated.
2. When three people are in the room, start a game of "Keep Away" using the ball or bean bag. Continue to play as others arrive. Put them with the group in the middle.
3. Stop the game but keep everyone standing in the "Keep Away" area. Ask, **Which do you prefer, the ends or the middle? What's the advantage of being an end? of being in the middle?**
Hand the "Child" placard to one end person, and the "Teenager" placard to the other end person. Ask, **How does it feel to be in the middle now, between a child and a teenager? What's the advantage of being in this middle?** Encourage a spirited discussion.
Ask, **What are you called in this middle? Who are you?** After a moment, say, **You have several names: preteen** (hand someone in the middle this placard), **preadolescent** (hand another this placard), **and my personal favorite, "tweenager"** (hand another this placard).
4. Discuss "tweenagers" being caught in the middle. Ask for volunteers to retrieve the childhood possession they brought with them and

explain why it's their favorite.

Say, **These favorite things you've brought remind you you're still a child. There are times you may feel more like a teenager.**

Place the "Child" and "Teenager" placards against opposite walls. Say, **I'm going to call out several words. If you feel more like a child when you hear each one, move to that wall. If you feel more like a teenager, move to that wall.** Be aware that the entire group may move to each wall as a group. Encourage individual thinking and expression. Here is the list:

- school (some are still in elementary school; some are in middle or junior high school)
- church (some sixth graders are in the youth group)
- your room
- your favorite books
- your favorite music
- your afterschool snacks

Give the group time to move after each phrase. Ask several to explain their moves and encourage discussion. Watch for those who move back and forth as examples of being caught in the middle of these two stages of life.

5. Divide the boys and girls, with the male coleader guiding the boys, and the female coleader guiding the girls.

Put the large newsprint in the middle of each circle and attach the strip "Timed to Grow" at the top. Ask children to read the first part of "My Growing—Understanding God's Timing," and "Built According to Plan" in the section of their book "My Feelings—Where Did They Come From?" Encourage their questions.

Have different ones read Jeremiah 29:11 and Luke 2:52. Discuss the importance of growing and changing according to God's plan.

Attach at the bottom of the newsprint the "Feeling High, Feeling Low" strip. Discuss the changes in feelings, too, and the importance of being honest with self and parents about them. Ask each group to cut out pictures, headlines, or slogans that show their high and low feelings about their physical and/or emotional changes.

6. Reassemble as one group and share the two posters. Post these and leave for the remaining sessions. Thank them for their lively participation. Dismiss with prayer.

Session 3
What I Think and See

Before the Session

1. Secure copies of many different types of magazines, including teen magazines. Spread them across a table near the room's entrance. Take

a long piece of newsprint and title it "Find an Ad For . . . ." Spaced over it put the words ". . . Cars," ". . . Movies," ". . . Perfume," ". . . Soap," ". . . Music," ". . . Anything to Drink." Mount the newsprint on the wall and have tape for securing ads to the newsprint.

2. Read "My Attitudes—My Business!" from *Sex! What's That?*

During the Session

1. As children gather, send them to a table covered with old magazines. Ask them to find and tear out examples of ads listed on your poster.

2. Talk about the ads on the poster. Ask the group: **Who is the ad trying to sell to? What is the message of the ad? Does its message match the product being sold?** Be ready to point out the subtle and not-so-subtle sexual messages in many ads they will find.

3. Assemble the group in a circle. Hand out a card and pencil to each child. Ask them to write down at least one sexual "fact" that their friends have taught them. Be ready to give a personal example to help them remember. Gather the cards. Selectively read a few of them and comment on whether or not the "fact" is actually a fact.

Pass out a second card. Ask the group, **If your only sexual information came from the "facts" I've just read and from the ads we've just discussed, what would you know about sex?** Again, take up the cards and selectively read a few. Help the group spot the attitudes being stated on the cards.

4. Load your group in cars or vans. (Before you do, get proper permission from parents as a safety precaution. Find out how your church handles trips—medical forms giving permission for emergency treatment, parental consent, etc.—and abide by them.) Explain that you are going on a driving scavenger hunt. Divide the following items among individuals or smaller groups to watch for or listen for during the drive. Remind them that you are trying to discover the sexual messages hidden in:

- billboards
- song lyrics on the radio
- ads on the radio
- headlines in a newspaper box
- dress of the people you see
- movie marquees
- bumper stickers
- T-shirts and sweatshirts

As you drive, talk about the power of suggestion in all of these media. Help your group understand that their sexual attitudes are formed by what they allow their eyes to see and their ears to hear. Unless they deliberately choose to have the same attitude about their sexuality that God does, their attitudes will become more and more like those of the world.

In a safe place, pull over. Ask one child to read Matthew 12:35. Ask the group how they can store up good attitudes about sex and their sexuality.

Then, have an adult read the story of Samuel's birth from 1 Samuel 1. Ask, **What kind of relationship did Samuel's parents have? What did Samuel's birth mean to them? What does this story teach us about God's purpose for sexuality? What attitudes do you think Samuel's parents had about God's gift of sexuality in their marriage?**

Finish the drive back to the meeting room.

Option: If you are unable to do the activity as described, have a discussion in your meeting room. Talk about and analyze song lyrics, movie themes, and some of the other things suggested for the scavenger hunt. Follow the discussion with the other plans recommended above.

5. Back in the meeting room, read Ephesians 2:10,22. Remind the group of God's presence in their lives and God's desire to live in us. Then, remind the group that God has that same desire for everyone else in the group and everyone else in the world. The key to matching our attitudes to God's attitudes is to think about ourselves and other people the way God does.

Close in prayer, asking God to make any attitude adjustments needed so that attitudes better reflect God and His way of looking at the world.

Session 4
What I Do 'Cause I'm Free

Before the Session

1. Read "My Actions—In Control and On Course!" in *Sex! What's That?*

2. Using specific bits of information from this chapter, design a set of clues hidden around the room. Each clue should have a true or false answer, and each answer should send the child to another hidden clue. If he makes all correct choices, the last clue should lead him to the circle of chairs. For example, one clue might read: "When God saw all that He created, He declared that it was good. True or False? If the answer is true, check under the chair closest to the window. If the answer is false, check under the nearest light switch." Of course there would be no clue under the light switch and the next clue would be under the chair.

3. Bring one or two copies of your most recent Sunday newspaper. Get two large sheets of newsprint.

4. Make large strips saying: "Wrong Place;" "Wrong Stuff;" "Wrong People."

During the Session

1. As children enter, show them the first clue and explain the object of finding the hidden clues—to choose the correct answers and to end up in the circle. As more children come, encourage early finishers to cheer for them. When everyone has had a try at the course, call time and form a group in the circle.

2. Debrief the opening activity. First, provide correct answers to the hidden clues. Let any children willing give answers. Help correct any misinformation which surfaces.

Ask, **What did you have to do to get from the door to the circle? What helped you stay on the right course?** (Good information; knowing the answers; following directions)

3. Give each child a section of the newspaper. Mount the two newsprint banners on a focal wall. Say, **Pretend that *all* we know about our world is in this newspaper. We want to find out if this is a rotten place to live or a super place to live. When you find a story or headline that convinces you the world is either rotten or super, tear it out and tape it on the correct banner.**

Call time after three minutes. Discuss the banners. Without any gory details, make it clear that much of our world is rotten. Use material from the opening paragraphs in this section of *Sex! What's That?* for a brief lecture about the world we live in and the sexual sins and mistakes that are found in it. Also emphasize that the world can be a super place when individuals make good choices. Remind them that in Genesis we read that when God saw the world He created, He declared that it was good.

4. Have the group stand in a straight line spaced far apart with eyes closed. Give them a series of simple commands (Take two giant steps forward; turn to your left; etc.). After eight or ten commands, let them open their eyes. Ask, **Is everyone in the same place now?** (They won't be.) **Everyone had the same directions; why aren't you all lined up like you started? What else do you need besides good directions to get where you want to be?**

5. Say, **We've thought a lot tonight about staying on course by following directions. You'll get off the course of God's best plan for your life if you're not careful in three areas.**

Mount the three sentence strips as you share materials from "Getting Off Course Can Happen If . . ." in the chapter.

6. Take time to deal with any final questions the group has given you to answer.

7. Write 1 Timothy 4:12 on a chalkboard. Ask the children to underline the five areas where young people can set an example to others (speech, conduct, love, faith, purity). Number off one to five around the circle, and group one's together, two's together, etc. Assign one of the five words in the passage to each group. Ask each group to think of three actions preadolescents can do that would set a good example.

8. Share group reports and affirm their suggestions. Use the five words again as the basis for a closing prayer.

Supplementary Group Study for Adolescents

Ann Cannon

This section is designed to equip church leaders to guide adolescents:
- To identify how their sexual growth affects other areas of life.
- To name several ways to develop an appropriate relationship with the opposite sex.
- To demonstrate responsible reactions to sexual pressures.
- To make a commitment to sexual purity.

Although recommended for four sessions, one session per week, the plans can be conducted over a period of six to eight weeks depending on the depth of discussion and the needs within the group.

Session 1
Body Talk

Before the Session

1. In addition to publicity for the adolescents, invite parents to the third group session. Urge parents to use the book *Sexuality: God's Gift* to work with their adolescents. Parents should encourage youth to bring their Bibles and books to each group session.

2. Provide a copy of *Sexuality: God's Gift* and pencil for each youth who forgets to bring one.

3. Prepare the "What If"assignments for Step 1.

4. Bring half sheets of paper for Step 2.

5. Make and display the signs, "Male," "Female," and "Both," for Step 3.

6. Prepare the continuum for Step 5 by writing each sexual activity on the list under "The Sexual Scene" in *Sexuality: God's Gift* on separate sheets of paper.

7. Read Chapter 1 in *Sexuality: God's Gift*.

During the Session

Grab Attention

1. Divide youth into teams of no more than five (same sex groups are more effective). Give each team one "What If" statement from Chapter

1 in *Sexuality: God's Gift*. Allow time for discussion, then ask each team to share its viewpoint. Say, **The "What If" statements look at sexual development from different angles. Let me challenge you to look at sex differently during these sessions than you would in a sex education class at school.**

Say, **During this session, we will look at sexual growth and how it influences all areas of our lives. Perhaps you feel like those "What If" statements—abnormal; really most of what is happening to you is normal.**

2. Say, **During these sessions we will address your fears, concerns, and questions.** Hand out the half-sheets of paper and pencils. Ask youth to write down no more than three questions they have about sex or any related area, including dating. Share a few topics to be covered in the other sessions.

Refer to youth's questions as you prepare the other sessions. These will help you meet their needs.

Gain Information

3. Hand out copies of *Sexuality: God's Gift* to each youth who needs a copy. Tell them to write their names on their books.

Ask a youth to read Psalm 139:14a from the Bible. Say, **We will look at how "fearfully and wonderfully" God made people as spiritual beings who have a sex—male or female.** Instruct each youth to complete the puzzle in "Understanding the Sexual Me" in Chapter 1, if they have not already done so at home.

As you check answers, form two groups; one for boys and the other for girls. In each group, explain why you use the correct terms for body parts, rather than slang. The answers are: (1) r; (2) h; (3) c; (4) u; (5) g; (6) n; (7) e; (8) f; (9) l; (10) i; (11) p; (12) v; (13) t; (14) j; (15) o; (16) m; (17) k; (18) b; (19) d; (20) s; (21) q; (22) a.

Use the illustrations in the *Sexuality: God's Gift* and the explanations to guide youth to understand each sexual function. Say, **The discomfort some people have in talking about sex is normal.**

4. Return to one group. Ask someone to read Genesis 1:27 from the Bible. Say, **When God made male and female, God created similarities and differences.** Point out the three previously made signs that say, "Male," "Female," and "Both." After you read each statement under "Male and Female" in the book, tell youth to walk to the appropriate sign. The answers are (1) male; (2) female; (3) male; (4) male; (5) both; (6) male; (7) female; (8) male; (9) female; (10) both; (11) female; (12) male.

Say, **The development of sex organs is only part of the story.** Explain how hormones influence emotions, feelings, and even actions.

5. Say, **God called His creation of male and female good.** Read Genesis 1:31a. Say, **God expects boys and girls to use their sexual organs only in the context of marriage.** Direct youth to 1 Thessalonians 4:3-7. Instruct them to read this passage silently, under-

lining specific statements that express God's desire for sexual purity.

After a few minutes, direct youth to find the verses that answer the questions in "The Sexual Scene" in *Sexuality: God's Gift*. This should have already been completed at home. (Possible answers are: (1) v. 3; (2) v. 5; (3) v. 6; (4) vv. 3 or 7.)

Say, **The one way to maintain sexual purity is to be aware of how the body reacts to sexual activity.** Place the sheets of paper prepared prior to the session on the floor in order, spreading them out to make a continuum.

Direct attention to the continuum. Explain, **A couple moves from one action to the next as they get more sexually involved. A person can move quickly from one situation to the next the further along the continuum you move. There is usually a point where it is difficult to stop.**

Direct youth, **Using the continuum, stand next to the statement that expresses where a person remains sexually pure, according to God's standards.**

Next, tell them, **Select the statement that expresses where society expects a teenager to stop.**

Finally, direct youth, **Walk to the statement that expresses how far they can go and remain sexually pure.**

Some youth may argue that sexual purity is preserved by anything that stops short of sexual intercourse. They may want permission to do everything up to that point. Respond that other actions actually cross the line of sexual purity. Emphasize the importance of choice and control.

Guide Into Action

6. Review the session's material by going over the true/false statements under "What's Happening?" in *Sexuality: God's Gift*. The answers are (1) false; (2) true; (3) false; (4) true; (5) true; (6) false; (7) false; (8) true; (9) true; (10) false.

Say, **Self-esteem plays an important role in sexuality.** Direct youth to complete the letter in "Some-Body: Construction in Progress" in *Sexuality: God's Gift*. Let volunteers share. Close with a prayer of thanksgiving for God's wonderful and fearful gift of sex.

Session 2
Male and Female—Isn't It Great!

Before the Session

1. Prepare the signs and cards for Step 1. You need two sets of signs, each set saying, "Healthy" and "Unhealthy." The two sets of cards should contain reasons for dating as listed in "The Dating Game" in Chapter 2 of *Sexuality: God's Gift*. Bring masking tape.

2. Bring a variety of magazines for Step 1.

3. Bring large sheets of paper and felt-tip markers for Steps 2 and 5.

4. Prepare the game for Step 3. Write each Bible reference and each statement from the matching activities in "Who Am I Sexually?" and "The Sex Part of Sexuality" in Chapter 2 of *Sexuality: God's Gift* on separate sheets of paper. Mix them up. Number them from 1 to 20 on the back.

5. Invite several older youth to serve on the panel in Step 4.

6. Read Chapter 2 in *Sexuality: God's Gift*.

During the Session

Grab Attention

1. Display the previously prepared sets of signs. Under each set, place a set of cards. Place masking tape circles nearby. Divide youth into two teams. Explain that you are looking for healthy and unhealthy reasons for dating (pointing to the headings). Tell one member of each team to race to their headings, pick up a card from their stack, place the card under the appropriate heading using the masking tape circle, and race back to tag the next team member. Continue the relay until all the cards have been used.

Evaluate each team's list. Compare responses to the answers in "The Dating Game."

Note that youth also think about an ideal date. Hand out magazines and instruct youth in pairs to build your perfect date. Guide them to find photos, words, or phrases out of the magazines that describe "your perfect date." After they have finished, allow them time to report to the group. Then ask, **What characteristics do you want in an ideal date?** List responses on a chalkboard. Direct youth to choose the top seven, in order of importance. Compare their responses to "My Ideal" in *Sexuality: God's Gift*.

Gain Information

2. Ask, **Do you think the opposite sex understands your gender?** In order to set the record straight, divide into teams of boys and girls. Give each team a large sheet of paper and a felt-tip marker. Tell them to make two lists. Say, **First, list what you would like to know about the opposite sex. Second, list what you wish the opposite sex knew about your gender.** If youth are immature, they may prefer to make a list of what society expects from their gender.

Share lists, discussing the differences. Remark, **God loves us even when others don't.**

3. To examine God's part in their sexuality, play a matching game. Use the sheets of paper prepared prior to the session. Place the sheets face down on the floor.

Using the same two teams from Step 1, instruct each team to turn over two sheets at a time to make a match between the Bible reference and the related statement. Urge them to use Bibles to look up the references.

If a team makes a match, they continue turning over two papers at a time until they miss. The team with the most match-ups wins. The answers for both match-ups are at the end of Chapter 2.

After the game, discuss how the statements affirm the goodness of God's creation of sex. Review God's purposes of sexual intercourse (pleasure, communication, and reproduction).

Guide Into Action

4. Describe how dating is part of the process that helps people become comfortable with their sexuality. Introduce the panel of older youth who can share ideas about dating. Ask, **When should a person start dating? How do you choose a date? What can you do on a date? What do you talk about on a date?** Let youth ask questions, too. Allow plenty of time for the panel.

After the panel discussion, review the true/false statements in Chapter 2 of *Sexuality: God's Gift*. The answers are (1) true; (2) false; (3) false; (4) true; (5) true; (6) true; (7) false; (8) true; (9) false; (10) true.

5. Let youth evaluate their personal relationship skills by working individually on the test in "Being Friends With the Opposite Sex" in the book. Help them score their tests and discover its meaning.

Based on this study, ask, **What are some ways you can get along with both sexes?** Write their responses on a large sheet of paper. Suggest they select one way to work on over the next few days. Pray for friendships.

Session 3
You're in Charge

Before the Session

1. Invite parents to attend this session.

2. Prepare and display the banner for Step 1. The banner reads, "Who is the world's greatest lover?"

3. Bring large sheets of paper and felt-tip markers for Step 2.

4. Enlist parents for the panel in Step 3.

5. Prepare the "Pressure Bag" for Step 6. Write on a piece of paper each pressure statement from the beginning of Chapter 3, as well as each statement under why some youth say yes to sexual intercourse and why others say no in "Just Say No And Mean It." Place these in a paper bag, labeled Pressure Bag.

6. Read Chapter 3 in *Sexuality: God's Gift*.

During the Session

Grab Attention

1. Direct attention to the previously prepared banner that says, "Who is the world's greatest lover?" Ask, **Who were some great lovers in**

history, in the Bible, and in movies, past and present? Who are great lovers today? What makes a great lover?

Say, **During this session we will look at what real love means. We will also examine reasons to remain sexually pure for the one who will be your future spouse.**

2. To discover the difference between love and lust, ask youth to identify the characteristics of each. List responses on a large sheet of paper. Compare this to the list in "In Love -vs- Sex Without Love?" in Chapter 3 of *Sexuality: God's Gift*. Ask, **How can a person tell the difference between being in love and being sexually aroused? That is a problem for youth who rely on feelings. Lust is only harmful when it gets out of hand.**

Gain Information

3. Propose that you are going to give youth a chance to rate their ability to be one of the world's greatest lovers. Direct them to "The World's Greatest Lovers" in the book. Call on someone to read 1 Corinthians 13:4-8a aloud. Ask youth to grade their own report cards.

Ask, **Where did you rate yourself high? Where did your rate yourself low? How do these qualities make a person a good lover?** Say, **True love requires more than sexual equipment or performance.**

Invite the enlisted parents to serve as a panel to discuss what love within marriage involves. Select representative home situations, including a single parent, a home where both parents work, a traditional home, a remarried couple, etc. Ask the panel, **What do you do on a daily basis that shows you love your spouse? How is married love different from love portrayed in the media? How did you know you were in love? How has your idea of love changed from the time you were dating?** Encourage youth to ask questions.

4. Say, **Neither sexual arousal, nor lust, nor love is a reason to have sex prior to marriage.** Divide youth and parents not on the panel into five teams. Divide into teams so that parents and their youth are on different teams. Assign each team a topic under "Truth and Consequences" in Chapter 3 of *Sexuality: God's Gift*. Tell teams to write a response to Ginny's letter at the end of "Truth and Consequences" using reasons for sexual purity related to their topic.

Call on teams to share their letters. Say, **Premarital sex can harm a marriage.** Explain why. Direct attention to the true-life stories in "Happily Ever After" in *Sexuality: God's Gift*. The parents' panel may also have comments.

Guide Into Action

5. Say, **Sometimes wrong actions feel right.** To help youth decide, point out the three tests of secrecy, universality, and prayer under "Just Say No And Mean It" in *Sexuality: God's Gift*. Encourage youth to underline these verses in their Bibles. Also, share how risky certain sit-

uations can be, like those discussed in "Know Your Limitations."

To review ideas about this session, do the true/false statements at the beginning of the Chapter 3. Number one is true; the rest are false.

6. Conclude the session by letting each youth practice responding to sexual pressure statements. Pass the Pressure Bag around that you prepared for this session. Tell each youth to take a slip of paper, decide if it's a positive or negative pressure, and state how they would respond. Continue until all slips have been evaluated.

Pray for God's help to say no to sexual temptation.

Session 4
Owner's Manual

Before the Session

1. Wrap a box as a gift for display during the session. Wrap the box so the top can be removed.

2. Prepare the myth signs for Step 1. Each sign should contain a myth from "Incorrect Product Information" in Chapter 4 of *Sexuality: God's Gift*.

3. Prepare the match-up cards for Step 3. These are three-by-five-cards on which you've written either the Bible reference or the Scripture truth from "Sex in the Bible" in the book.

4. Bring three-by-five-inch cards and pencils to be used in Step 6.

5. Read Chapter 4 in *Sexuality: God's Gift*.

During the Session

Grab Attention

1. Place the previously wrapped box in the center of the room. Around the room, hang the previously prepared myth signs. Place a few chairs under each sign. Instruct youth, **Decide whether the statement where you are seated is true or false and why. Refer to** *Sexuality: God's Gift* **for information.**

Say, **Often youth get incorrect or partially correct information from peers and the media.** Ask, **What other myths or misinformation have you heard?** Answer any questions from previous sessions that have gone unanswered.

Point out that in this session youth will put together the information they've been studying.

Gain Information

2. Say, **People use the phrase "I love you" to mean different things.** Direct youth to the three ways it is stated in "Operate With Caution." Ask youth to respond verbally to what the sentence means with the different words emphasized. Ask, **How can you show someone you love that person other than saying the words?** In addition

to youth's ideas, point out the ideas under "Operate With Caution" in *Sexuality: God's Gift.*

3. Say, **Although the Bible may not have a specific answer for each dating or sexual question, it does have universal truths.** Give each youth a match-up card you prepared earlier. Ask youth to look up their references and mingle until they find the person with the card containing the related truth. The match-up answers are at the end of Chapter 3 in *Sexuality: God's Gift.*

Review these truths. Ask, **Which truth will help you with dating? Which truth can help you with sexual temptation?**

4. To review the reasons for staying pure, let youth work in the pairs formed in Step 3. Ask pairs to unscramble the words in "Why Stay Pure?" Ask, **Which reason do you think is the strongest for remaining pure? Which is the weakest? Which reason is most likely to help you stay pure? Why?**

5. Say, **While God made sexuality and sex good, people mess it up.** Briefly review the sexual misuses in "Product Misuse" in the book. Ask, **How do you feel about these sexual misuses?**

Divide into four teams. Assign each team a case study from "Product Misuse." Instruct teams to prepare a brief role play to respond to the related questions. Share role plays.

Ask, **Have any of you had any experience like these personally or with a friend? How did you handle it?** Encourage them to offer hope and help to their friends who have experienced these sexual situations.

Guide into Action

6. Review this session by doing the true/false statements in Chapter 4. The answers are (1) true; (2) false; (3) true; (4) true; (5) false; (6) true; (7) true; (8) false; (9) false; (10) false.

Explain, **These sessions were designed to give you sexual information, as well as moral reasons for remaining pure. We hope that you have found reasons to select sexual purity.**

Direct attention to the incomplete sentences in "All You Ever Wanted to Know About Sex, But Were Afraid to Ask" in the book. Hand out the three-by-five-inch cards. Encourage youth to either write out the commitment card from *Sexuality: God's Gift* or complete a sentence from the "All You Ever Wanted to Know About Sex, But Were Afraid to Ask" section on the card. Ask youth to place their cards in the gift box as their gift to God.

Say, **God has given you a wonderful gift in sex. What you do with that gift is up to you for the rest of your lives.**

Say, **God forgives past sexual sins when repentance is genuine. I want to help youth understand God's forgiveness, and can meet with you privately at any time.** Read Romans 12:2 from the Bible. Pray for strength to hold on to God's standards.

Glossary

Abortion: termination of pregnancy at any stage.

Adolescence: the period of life between childhood and adulthood, from the time of puberty to maturity; about ages 13 to 20 although some physiologists view changes which occur until about age 24 as being indicative of a longer period of time.

Adultery: voluntary sexual intercourse between a married person and someone other than his or her legal spouse.

AIDS: Acquired Immune Deficiency Syndrome, a physical problem when the body's natural defenses against disease and infection are destroyed. The AIDS virus, known as human immunodeficiency virus, or HIV, can so weaken a person's immune system that he or she cannot fight off even mild infections. The AIDS virus is transmitted through the exchange of infected body fluids. Many homosexuals and heterosexuals are infected with the virus through oral or anal sex and promiscuity, but many others are infected through unscreened blood transfusions or through contaminated needles used for the injection of drugs. The virus can also be transferred to the unborn baby in the mother's womb if she is an HIV carrier.

Amniotic fluid: the fluid in which the unborn child "floats" in the womb of the mother until birth, cushioned against bumps, shocks, and damage.

Anatomy: the science of the structure and parts of the body; the structure of the body itself.

Artificial insemination: introduction of the male semen into the vagina or womb of a woman by artificial means; this is done when intercourse is not possible or because of other physical difficulties.

Birth: when the baby leaves its mother's body and enters the outside world.

Birth canal: the way by which the baby enters the world, it drops down in the womb, passes through the cervix to the vagina.

Birth control: controlling how many children a couple will have or when the children will be conceived by controlling conception through the use of condoms, diaphragms, IUDs, drugs, or rhythm method.

Ceasarean birth (section): delivery of a baby through a surgical incision rather than through the birth canal.

Castration: removal of the testicles in the male or ovaries in the woman, the result being the inability to bear children.

Cervix: the neck of the uterus which is the passageway between the uterus and the vagina.

Christian sex education: the continuous process of guiding preschoolers, children, youth, and adults to understand the emotional, physical, intellectual, social, and spiritual aspects of development and their interrelatedness to the development of a healthy sexuality based on a set of values consistent with biological factors and biblical teachings.

Chromosome: a structure within the cells which carry the genes. Each cell in the body contains 46 chromosomes except the sex cells which carry 23 each.

Circumcision: an operation performed on boys to remove part of the foreskin of the penis; this is usually done for religious reasons or medical (hygienic) purposes within a few days of birth.

Clitoris: the very sensitive small organ of the female, just inside the upper end of the vulva; it is covered by a fold of skin and for some women is an important point of reaching sexual climax.

Conception: the union of the female ovum with the male sperm; this produces an embryo which grows into a baby.

Condom: a contraceptive used by the male; it is a sheath which fits over the penis and prevents semen from entering the vagina.

Congenital trait: a characteristic acquired by a baby before or at birth which is not inherited through the genes such as a physical deformity or disease.

Contraception: a way to prevent conception.

Ejaculation: the discharge of seminal fluid from the penis; also known as an emission.

Embryo: an unborn child, from conception to about three months in the mother's womb. (See fetus.)

Erection: the swelling and becoming rigid and erect of the penis when blood rushes into the penis when sexually aroused. For the pre-teen and teenager, this may occur when the boy least expects it and may be a source of intense embarrassment. The erection will usually relax if the young person can think about something else or get busy with something.

Estrogen: the female sex hormone.

Exceptional children: children who have physical, mental, and/or emotional limitations or giftedness.

Dysfunctional family: a family that has impaired relationships or is caught up in abnormal behavior for one or more reasons (i.e., drugs, alcohol, sexual and/or physical abuse) to the detriment of one or more family members or society.

Fallopian tubes: tubes which extend from the ovaries to the uterus; they are the way by which the ovum travels to the uterus and fertilization of the egg usually occurs in one of the tubes.

Fertilization: the joining of an egg cell and a sperm.

Fetus: an unborn child, from about three months in the mother's womb until birth. (See embryo.)

Foreskin: the cap of skin over the penis which is often removed by surgery. (See circumcision.)

Fornication: sexual intercourse between two consenting, unmarried persons.

Gene: a tiny unit on the chromosomes which determine the characteristics of the baby.

Genitals: the sex organs of the body.

Gestation: the period of time from conception to birth.

Gland: organs which release chemical substances into the blood stream; the endocrine glands secrete hormones, potent chemicals with specific actions.

Gonads: the organs which form and nurture the reproductive cells. In women they take the form of ovaries and in men they are the testes.

Heredity: the transmission of traits from parents to children.

Heterosexual: a person whose desire and preference in sexual relations is with someone of the opposite sex.

Homosexual: a person whose desire and preference in sexual relations is with someone of the same sex.

Hormone: chemical substances which affect activity and growth in and of the body.

Hymen: the thin membrane which partly covers the opening of the vagina in most girls. It is more like a tire-shaped membrane with an opening in the middle for the passage of menstrual discharge rather than a complete covering. The absence of a hymen does not necessarily prove lack of virginity in that the hymen can be stretched by many different kinds of activity.

Infertility: the inability of couples to have children; this may be a problem with the man, the woman, or both.

Incest: sexual relations between close relatives such as father or mother with a child.

Lesbian: a female homosexual.

Masturbation (self-pleasuring): self-stimulation of sexually sensitive parts of the body to produce sexually pleasurable feelings.

Menstruation (period): a shedding of the uterine lining through the vagina; this normally occurs about every 28 days and lasts from 3-5 days.

Middle-aged childhood: as used in the Christian Sex Education resources, the period of childhood development around the ages of eight to nine.

Miscarriage: the loss (spontaneous abortion) of the baby before it is old enough to live outside the mother's body.

Navel: the place on the abdomen where the baby was joined to the umbilical cord during prenatal life.

Orgasm (climax): the intense sensation that occurs at the peak of sexual stimulation.

Ovaries: the two reproductive glands of the female which produce egg cells and certain hormones.

Ovulation: the production of ripe eggs from the ovaries.

Ovum: the egg or egg cell which the woman produces every month.

Penis: the male sex organ that projects outside the body; this is the organ through which sperm cells and urine leave the body, although not at the same time.

Placenta: the special lining of the uterus during pregnancy which provides nourishment for the baby and for the disposal of its body wastes.

Preadolescence: the time immediately preceding adolescence, usually around the ages of 10 to 13 just before puberty.

Pregnant: condition of a female expecting a child, during which a single cell is transformed into a human being within the female body; this period of time lasts about 270 days.

Premature birth: birth which occurs before 38 weeks gestation.

Prenatal: this refers to the period prior to birth of a child.

Puberty: sexual maturity when the organs mature and become capable of reproduction. This occurs at about 12 years of age for girls and at about 14 years of age for boys, although it can be earlier.

Rape: sexual intercourse which is forced on an individual without consent.

Rhythm method: a method of birth control; this relies upon keeping a calendar of a woman's cycle and not having intercourse during her fertile period.

Scrotum: the pouch of skin behind (below) the penis which contains the male testes.

Semen: the thick fluid that carries the sperm of the man; it is ejected from the penis when a man reaches orgasm.

Seminal emission (nocturnal emission, wet dream): the discharge of semen during sleep; it is a natural way of controlling the build-up of semen in adolescent boys.

Sexual intercourse: the union of male and female in which the penis is inserted into the vagina.

Sperm: tiny, microscopic cells, produced by the male; when one combines with the female egg, it fertilizes the egg and starts a new life.

Sterility: the inability to produce offspring.

Testes: the two male reproductive glands which are enclosed in the scrotum; they manufacture sperm cells and the male sex hormones. Also known as testicles.

Testicles: (See testes.)

Twins: babies born at the same time; may be fraternal or identical. Fraternal twins develop from two separate eggs and have the same relationship with each other as any sibling in that they may be of the same or opposite sex and may look alike or quite different. Identical twins develop from a single fertilized ovum which splits into two parts. These babies will be the same sex and look almost alike.

Umbilical cord: a thick, rope-like cord which connects the baby to the placenta and through which the unborn baby gets everything it needs.

Uterus: the chamber where a baby develops before birth. It is also known as the womb.

Vagina: the passageway from the outside of the woman's body to the uterus and the place where sperm cells are deposited during intercourse.

Vulva: the two pairs of "lips" forming the outside part of the female sex organ and the entrance to the vagina.

Womb: (See uterus.)

Young childhood: as used in Christian Sex Education resources, the period of childhood development around the ages of four to seven.

Additional Resources

The following list contains books, video tapes, and audio cassette tapes that provide helpful additional material for you and for your child. In all cases, preview a resource to judge the appropriateness of the material for his or her particular needs before you give it to your child. Not all of these resources will contain material consistent with your attitudes, values, and beliefs; however, each book will have sections that will prove to be helpful in a solid knowledge base and in methodology of sex education. It is good for you to be familiar with what is current in sex education to better understand the importance of your need to take a leading role in this aspect of your child's upbringing.

Several of the resources included in this list are about child sexual abuse. Sexual abuse is one area of sex education that is often glossed over with the belief by many adults that it won't happen to their child. Such a head-in-the-sand approach is to be deplored. Much more information is needed for all adults.

About Sex and Growing Up. Evelyn Duvall. Association Press. A comprehensive book for elementary age children, it covers the moral aspect of sex as well as the facts.

Come Tell Me Right Away. Linda Sanford. Fayetteville, NY: Ed-U Press, Inc., 1982. A condensed version of an earlier book by the same author called "The Silent Children," this booklet is about the prevention of child sexual abuse.

From Parent to Child About Sex. Wilson Wayne Grant. Grand Rapids, MI: Zondervan Press, 1973. A Christian view of what sex education for children should be and how information and views on sex should be transmitted to children.

Generation to Generation: Communicating Christian Views About Sexuality in the Home and Church. Lane and Bob Powell. Dallas: Baptist General Convention of Texas, 1991. A video-based curriculum to assist parents and youth in communicating about sexuality. Six sessions contained in a 120 minute video tape.

He Told Me Not to Tell. King County Rape Relief. Renton, WA. A 30-

page booklet on what to tell children about incest. (King County Rape Relief, 305 S. 43rd St., Renton, WA 98055).

How to Know You're in Love. Dawson McAllister. Waco, TX: Word, Inc. A 67 minute video presentation on love-vs-infatuation from a strong biblical, Christian perspective. Presented in a lecture format, the video is intended for home use.

No More Secrets. Caren Adams and Jennifer Fay. San Luis Obispo, CA, 1981. A book written to help parents know how to protect their children from sexual assault.

Parent's Guide to Christian Conversation About Sex. Erwin Kolb. Concordia Publishing House. A book to help parents answer children's questions on an appropriate level.

Parents Talk Love. Susan Sullivan and Matthew Kawiak. New York: Bantam Books, 1984. A book to show parents how to take responsibility for their child's sexual education. It looks at a child's sexual development, some common myths and misconceptions in sexual knowledge, and how to deal with tough issues such as homosexuality and pornography.

Preventing Child Sexual Abuse. Mary Nelson and Kay Clark (Eds.). Santa Cruz, CA: Network Publications, 1986. The complete title of the book is "An Educator's Guide to Preventing Child Sexual Abuse," and it is a comprehensive book on issues, guidelines for prevention, and resources.

Raising PG Kids in an X-Rated Society. Tipper Gore. Nashville: Abington Press, 1987. Explicit material. This book fully informs parents about the irresponsible excesses of the entertainment industry, and provides practical guidance in protecting children and youth from its influences.

Raising Positive Kids in a Negative World. Zig Ziglar. New York: Ballentine Books, 1985; four-part video series published by Thomas Nelson Publishers; six-part audio cassette series published by The Zig Ziglar Corporation. Deals with the need for and the responsibility of parents to instill positive self esteem in their children. Chapter 14 addresses sex education in the home as an imperative for raising positive children.

Raising Sexually Healthy Children. Lynn Leight. New York: Avon Books, 1988. Written by a sex counselor and nurse for parents wishing for natural communication with children on the subject of sex.

Sex and the Family. James C. Dobson. Waco, TX: Word, Inc. A 60 minute, three-part video intended for home use. Part 1 deals with the when, why, and how of explaining sex to children. Part 2 encourages the traditional view that boys should be taught to be masculine and girls to be feminine. Part 3 is a frank discussion of common sexual problems experienced in marriage and is not recommended for young children.

Teens Speak Out: "What I Wish My Parents Knew About My Sexuality." Josh McDowell. San Bernadino, CA: Here's Life Publishers, 1987. A compilation of the thoughts of evangelical Christian teenagers gathered from surveys, questionnaires, group and personal interviews, response sheets, and essays. Excellent, practical reasons are given regarding why teens should remain sexually pure until marriage. See additional "Why Wait?" resources listed later.

The Dating Book. Lane Powell. Nashville: Convention Press, 1989. Helps youth develop confidence in responding to dating issues and experiences by considering dating behaviors and attitudes consistent with Christian life-styles.

The Hurried Child: Growing Up Too Fast Too Soon. David Elkind. New York: Addison-Wesley, 1981. A book that reminds parents and educators of the importance of letting children experience childhood.

The 24-Hour Counselor Series. Richard Ross, compiler. Nashville: Broadman Press, 1987-92. These audiocassettes offer professionally competent, clinically-based advice to hurting youth and their parents in a form they will accept and understand.
  Volume 1 Helps youth who feel lonely, want to stop drinking, doubt their salvation, or are involved with other problems.
  Volume 2 Helps deal with issues like sexual abuse, guilt, depression, dating, divorce, and more.
  Volume 3: Parent Edition Helps parents know how to respond to their youth's sexual activity, privacy demands, and other problems.
  Volume 4: Youth Doubt Edition Helps youth grapple with subjects ranging from their personal spiritual life to the reality of God.
  The 24-Hour Counselor Capsule Series Separate tapes with each dealing with one specific subject. Tapes include Depression, Abuse, Suicide, Date Rape, Adoption, and Shame-Bound Experiences.
  The 24-Hour Counselor series is also available for African American youth and Hispanic youth in separate albums they will accept and understand.

What's Happening to Me? Peter Mayle. Secaucus, NJ: Lyle Stuart, Inc., 1973. This book addresses the changes which take place at puberty and is written and illustrated in the same way as "Where Did I Come From?"

Where Did I Come From? Peter Mayle. Secaucus, NJ: Lyle Stuart, Inc., 1973. This is a non-threatening book about the facts of life. It is introduced with cartoon-like illustrations and the text is handled lightly, but thoroughly.

Why Wait? What You Need to Know About the Teen Sexuality Crisis. Josh McDowell and Dick Day. San Bernadino, CA: Here's Life Publishers, 1987. Offers excellent material on the reasons teens say "yes" to sex, and counters them with positive, biblical principles to protect themselves, and to provide for themselves physically, spiritually, emotionally, and relationally. Aimed at helping parents know how to effectively help their children say "no" to sexual pressures.

Why Wait Series for Junior and Senior High School Youth. Barry St. Clair and Bill Jones. Josh McDowell, series editor. San Bernadino, CA: Here's Life Publishers, 1987. A three-book series:
   Love: Making It Last
   Sex: Desiring the Best
   Dating: Picking (and Being) a Winner
There is also a parent's book to support the series: *Talking with Your Kids About Love, Sex, and Dating*. Published in 1989.

Why Wait Videos. Josh McDowell. The following videos support the Why Wait series. Published by Word, Inc., Waco, TX.
   The Myths of Sex Education. 45 minutes
   Why Waiting Is Worth the Wait. 30 minutes
   Let's Talk About Love and Sex. 35 minutes
   No! The Positive Answer. 60 minutes
   How to Teach Your Child to Say "No" to Sexual Pressure. Two 60 minute video tapes, a 23 minute audio cassette tape, and a book.

Wonderfully Made. Ruth Hummel. Concordia Publishing House. A book for children, ages nine to eleven about sexual growth.

The Way Your Body Works. Bernard Stonehouse. New York: Crown Publishers, 1974. An exceptionally well-written, carefully documented, and nicely illustrated book on the human body.